THE PROACTIVE
PROFESSIONAL

THE PROACTIVE PROFESSIONAL

HOW TO STOP PLAYING CATCH UP AND START GETTING AHEAD AT WORK
(AND IN LIFE!)

Chrissy Scivicque

ISBN: 0692755209
ISBN 13: 9780692755204
Library of Congress Control Number: 2016911452
CCS Ventures, LLC, Atlanta, GA

The Proactive Professional
How to Stop Playing Catch Up and Start Getting Ahead at Work (and in Life!)

Chrissy Scivicque
Founder of Eat Your Career
Helping You Create a Nourishing Professional Life
www.EatYourCareer.com
A Division of CCS Ventures, LLC

For Mom
My most enthusiastic supporter and compassionate critic, whose faith
encouraged me to always keep writing.

CONTENTS

GREETINGS

MY NAME IS Chrissy Scivicque. Don't let that last name scare you; it's easier than it looks. I think my ancestors wanted to look fancy, but really, it's pronounced like "civic." If you want to be proper, put the emphasis on the end. I also recommend using an exaggerated accent of your choice just for fun.

Now that I've addressed the question I hear most frequently, allow me to take a stab at the next one you might be pondering: *Who exactly is this Chrissy person?*

Broadly speaking, I consider myself a Learning and Development specialist. I've devoted my career to helping others achieve success in theirs. My primary role is that of corporate trainer. However, I'm also a career coach, public speaker, curriculum designer, and writer. You might have seen my work in the careers section of *U.S. News & World Report* or on Forbes. com, CBS News, CareerBuilder, Monster, or any of a dozen other major publications and websites.

Maybe my work is totally unknown to you, and that's cool too.

I also proudly label myself an enthusiastic and tireless researcher. I spend the majority of my time exploring what drives success in the workplace. And I take special joy in building new frameworks and models to help people understand and leverage these concepts in their own lives.

I'd like to invite you to connect with me online through my website and blog, www.EatYourCareer.com. That's a weird name, I know, but it's actually based on one of my favorite success frameworks. The whole idea behind "Eat Your Career" is that I truly believe work can be a delicious, *nourishing* life experience. The bigger purpose in my work is to help people discover what that means for them and how to achieve it. When you do it right, I believe your career can add tremendous value to your life.

This book, along with all of the other tools and resources available on my website, will help you contribute more value as a professional. In my experience, there's a direct correlation between what you contribute and what you receive—in both tangible and intangible terms. I believe your experience after reading *The Proactive Professional* will be the same. Please tell me about it by sending an email to Chrissy@EatYourCareer. com and share it with others by leaving an Amazon review.

Thank you for choosing to invest in yourself by reading this book. I've worked very hard to make it worth your time.

PART 1

INTRODUCTION

CHAPTER 1

WHY BOTHER?

As a professional, you've probably experienced any number of "bad days." Maybe they went something like this...

- You sit down for a meeting with colleagues, and the conversation is totally over your head. Apparently, everyone else did some pre-meeting research on their own—and some even made notes for discussion! As your colleagues jump right into business, you struggle to get up to speed.

- You're hosting an important training session online, but as you go to log in, you realize your computer system is missing a critical application required to launch the meeting. It takes twenty-five minutes and a phone call to tech support before you're finally able to get started. By that point, your participants have already given up, and you have to reschedule the training.

- You put off an important project, knowing it shouldn't take long to complete. However, as the deadline approaches, you encounter tons of unexpected setbacks and delays. Before you know it, the deadline has passed, and you're left trying to explain what happened.

What do all these situations have in common?

First, they're typical in today's working world, so don't beat yourself up if they hit close to home. Second, they're frustrating, stressful, embarrassing, and potentially career damaging. But here's the good news: situations like these are also completely within your control.

If you've ever experienced something similar to any of the bad day scenarios above, you likely also experienced a moment of clarity where you thought to yourself, "I wish I had done something different *before*..."—a month ago, a week ago, an hour ago. If only you had prepped for the meeting, tested the technology, started the project sooner...

If only you had spent a little time in the past preparing for the possibilities of the future, your present would be a whole lot better.

With the benefit of hindsight, it's easy to see the problems that arise when you procrastinate and fail to think ahead. These kinds of situations are telltale signs of professionals who are always playing *catch up*—a game that ensures they'll never get ahead and which keeps them constantly blindsided by the events and circumstances life throws their way.

The fascinating part is that most of these things are predictable and preventable—or at the very least, made more manageable—with the help of a skillset called *proactivity*. Being proactive gives us the power not only to deal more effectively with life but to actually take an active role in creating it.

Pretty amazing stuff.

The situations described in the opening to this chapter are relatively insignificant. Most people would find them irritating but would likely recover quickly. I could share many other stories that have far more serious consequences.

Take, for example, my former client Julie, who, after sixteen years working for the same organization, arrived at work one day to discover her department and her job had been eliminated. Suddenly unemployed at fifty-three years old, Julie couldn't even find a copy of her old, outdated résumé. When she came to me, her skills were nearly obsolete for her field (she hadn't engaged in any professional development in years), and her network had shrunk to include only a handful of former colleagues at the now-downsized company. In short, Julie had become complacent, and it came back to bite her.

Stories like this sadden me because things didn't have to be so hard for Julie. But I assure you, after this experience and after our work together, Julie will never be blindsided again. She will always be well positioned for her future, whatever that may bring. From now on, she will always be the driver of her own destiny.

Obviously, we don't always know what the future holds, and we can't always stop bad things from happening. But we can always make smart decisions today to prepare for the possibilities of the future, and we can take an active role in creating the kind of future we want.

When you're trapped in the tyranny of today, focused solely on the here and now, it can be hard to break out of the cycle. Like Julie, you get comfortable in your day-to-day routine. You're so busy staring down at the road immediately in front of you that you never bother to look around and make sure you're still on the right path. You begin to believe you know exactly what to expect, even though you really have no idea. You fail to adjust for changes ahead, and as a result, you're constantly caught off guard by every little bump or curve in the road.

I presume you're reading this book because you don't like that feeling. Perhaps you're also unhappy with the results you're getting. Put another way, the road you're on isn't leading to the right place, and the journey itself is pretty tedious.

Learning to be proactive doesn't mean the road will always be smooth. Bumps and curves will still happen, but you'll be more prepared when they do. More importantly, you'll discover that you're actually even in charge of them. *When you're proactive, your choices and actions dictate the path—not the other way around.*

If this sounds a bit abstract, don't worry. All the pieces of the puzzle will fall into place, I assure you. When they do, that feeling of playing catch up will disappear. You'll feel more empowered and more in control. And you'll finally get ahead at work and in life.

LEARNING TO LOVE PROACTIVITY

I've always been fascinated by the word *proactive*. Long before it was a best-selling acne face wash, *proactive* was a favorite buzzword for many business professionals, including my former boss. Many times a day, you could find him, perched on the edge of someone's desk, extolling the virtues of being proactive.

Unfortunately, he used the word with such frequency I began to question my understanding of it. Has that ever happened to you? A word that used to make sense suddenly sounds foreign when repeated over and over again? That's what happened to me with *proactive*.

So I set off on a research project. My goal originally was to understand the concept of being proactive, but I quickly learned the term's complexity. Over time, my goal grew. I not only wanted to understand it; I wanted to define a process for developing it—something that would work for me as well as the millions of other professionals who struggled with proactivity—and I wanted to establish practical strategies for applying this skill in the workplace.

This is how I began what I now consider my ten-year love affair with pro-activity. It's also a perfect demonstration of why my current career as a corporate trainer is a perfect fit for me. After all, who else would admit to having love affairs with concepts?

As a learning professional, this kind of thing excites me. Nothing is more thrilling than unpacking a complicated idea and really getting to know it. Nothing is more challenging than designing models for helping everyday professionals develop and integrate new skills in the workplace. And nothing is more satisfying than inspiring those "aha" moments when learners suddenly grasp a difficult topic with a brand new, almost magical level of clarity.

One of the first things I learned in my research project was that most professionals are the exact opposite of proactive—they're *reactive*. Most people habitually wait for life to happen to them, and then they react to it. They're passengers along for the ride, rather than drivers sitting at the wheel.

Taking the proactive approach requires a deep shift that can impact all areas of life. It involves recognizing and harnessing your own power to create your experiences. It's a matter of personal responsibility— something many people are surprisingly willing (and even eager) to relinquish, especially in the workplace.

Being reactive is costly, stressful, time wasting, and dangerously ineffective. The typical reactive professional experiences a number of frustrations. Here are just a few of the common complaints I hear from clients and classroom participants before completing my proactivity training sessions. See if any sound familiar to you.

- I feel like I'm always playing catch up and never getting ahead.
- I'm totally focused on what's going on today; I never have time to think about tomorrow.
- I'm often surprised by what's in front of me each day.

- I feel overwhelmed by unexpected issues that come up.
- I face the same challenges and frustrations over and over again.
- I know some problems are predictable, but I often miss the signs.
- I know some problems are preventable, but I often fail to take action in time.
- I often miss deadlines or find myself rushing to meet them at the last minute.
- I feel powerless over everything around me—like I don't have control over my day-to-day circumstances.
- I know I'm not working as effectively as I could, but I don't know what I'm doing wrong.

Learning to be proactive helps resolve all of these issues and more. It is, in my opinion, the one thing that separates the average professional from the exceptional one—*in any position, in any industry.*

Whether you're a salesperson or a customer service agent, an administrative professional or graphic designer, an entrepreneur or executive—regardless of what you do for a living, being proactive is the most essential (and most underutilized) tool for professional empowerment and personal productivity.

The proactive professional is always thinking about the future, planning and preparing for what lies ahead. He or she takes action today to make tomorrow better. As a result, the proactive professional

- makes better use of resources, including time, energy, and money;
- prevents problems from occurring;
- responds promptly and appropriately to problems that can't be avoided, thus reducing their negative impact;
- feels a greater sense of control and experiences less stress;

- establishes a positive and powerful reputation. (In fact, the proactive professional is often described as a *problem solver, strategic thinker, self-starter,* and even *practically clairvoyant!*)

Learning to be proactive can and will change who you are as a professional. It will make your life and the lives of the people you work with and for easier. It will make you more effective and more efficient. In short, you will become a more valuable asset for any organization. It is truly a key that unlocks amazing career potential.

These are audacious claims, I know, but I've experienced all of these promises (and more) in my own life.

In fact, I'll never forget the first time my former boss (the one who got me so fascinated with the topic in the first place) complimented my proactivity prowess. He had just asked me to complete a task for him with a deadline for the following afternoon.

In response to his request, I said smoothly, "I already did it. It's on your desk."

For a moment, he was speechless. Then a big smile broke out over his face, and he said the words I had been longing to hear.

"You read my mind!" he joked. "Thanks for getting ahead of that."

I realized then that "getting ahead" of something is code for "being proactive," and it felt so good.

Of course, that's just one example of hundreds from my own life. Over time in that position, I gained more responsibility, more respect, and more recognition as a valuable contributor to the organization—my paycheck, title, and reputation reflected this as well.

Today, as an entrepreneur and a corporate trainer, I've continued to reap the rewards of proactivity. In my line of business, things don't go perfectly the vast majority of the time. (Perhaps you can relate?) It's typical to arrive at a venue for speaking engagements, for example, and find there's no projector for displaying slides or the room is configured all wrong.

When these things happen, I don't get frantic, frazzled, and frustrated like many of my colleagues. Instead, I'm prepared; I always have a contingency plan. But I also find that things *do* tend to go according to plan more often for me because I've thought them through—I've pre-empted the typical *surprises* that frequently throw others off. And when the unavoidable problems happen, I have a greater ability to handle them with grace.

But don't take my word for it. Here are just a few of the extraordinary results my clients have experienced and shared with me after implementing the practices and processes outlined in this book.

- "I no longer live with that sinking feeling that I forgot to do something. I *know* I'm on top of my work and my life responsibilities."
- "Problems still happen, but much less frequently, and I'm more prepared to handle them—and they're no longer my fault!"
- "A lot of things at work are outside my control, but I *feel* more in control now. There's a whole new level of clarity I never had before."
- "My entire approach to work has changed for the better. Even my boss agrees!"

It's impossible to count how many crises have been prevented or minimized with the help of proactivity. We can't count the time or dollars saved with any real accuracy, though many of my students estimate their productivity has increased anywhere between 25 to 50 percent. This would sound unbelievable to me if I didn't already know the power of what we're talking about here.

But we do know with certainty the psychological impact of being proactive—reduced stress, a greater sense of control, and an overall feeling of empowerment.

Sounds enticing, doesn't it? If you're ready to unleash your own proactivity prowess, keep reading.

CHAPTER 2

HOW TO USE THIS BOOK

IN THE SPIRIT of being proactive, I want to warn you from the outset that this book covers a lot of territory. My goal in writing was to be as comprehensive as possible without overwhelming you, dear reader.

To be clear, this book is designed to be read one page at a time from beginning to end. Sounds obvious, I realize, but in today's high-tech world full of bite-sized information, people aren't necessarily accustomed to this kind of reading. They're tempted to flip ahead and skip around.

Please don't give in to that temptation. Instead, read the book from cover to cover first. Then, as you begin to implement what you've learned, feel free to bounce around as much as you'd like and as you see fit.

The book is divided into three parts: (1) Introduction, (2) The Proactive Skillset, and (3) Conclusion. Obviously, part 2 is where most of the meat is, but the parts on either side provide helpful context.

I hope you'll continue to use this book as a reference tool forever. I believe there is no greater compliment one can pay to a writer than to dog-ear, highlight, and underline the pages of a book until it's practically destroyed.

You'll probably find some of the strategies contained here intuitive, while others may sound completely foreign. Remember that the idea of proactivity has been around for a long time, but it's never before been broken down like this into an actionable framework. For most people, brand new concepts are challenging to accept, so I ask you to approach with an open mind.

While you read, you may hear a little voice in the back of your head saying something like, "Yeah, but..." followed by one excuse or another for why the strategies you're reading about won't work for you. I get it. I'm a skeptic too. In fact, I love it when people openly express doubt and resistance to my ideas. It helps me consider different perspectives, encourages me to re-evaluate what I'm sharing, and ultimately helps improve my work.

I've heard many "Yeah, buts" while presenting this topic in the past. This is why I've included a specific section under this heading at the end of each chapter in part 2 to address the most common points of resistance. Whenever you hear that little suspicious voice in the back of your head, hold that thought. I'm confident that most of your misgivings will subside as you continue reading.

Also at the end of each chapter in part 2, you'll find an area called "Reflection Exercises." These questions and short "assignments" will help you think more deeply about what you've just read and how the concepts apply to your own life and work. Personally, I enjoy this kind of thing. I hope you do as well and that you find the reflection process enlightening.

Finally, I want to address the examples contained in this book. I believe stories are one of the most powerful tools for learning, which is why I use them liberally. I always change the names of real-world people for confidentiality reasons.

To make life easy, I've also created two recurring characters to star in many of our examples. Their names are Proactive Patty and Reactive Rita.

Both Patty and Rita are constructions; they are not real people. However, they are composites of *many* real professionals, both male and female. I'm not a scientist. I don't test my ideas in lab-like conditions; I don't use finely controlled social experiments. Patty and Rita are based on people I've known—some colleagues, some clients—and people I've observed in the real world. I find that using these caricatures helps protect both the innocent and the guilty.

I've done my best to make the stories as relatable as possible by removing specifics associated with the role and business in which Patty and Rita work. That being said, if you're looking for a reason to say, "These people are nothing like me!" you'll probably find it. Again, I ask you to quiet your inner skeptic, open your mind, and look for similarities.

On occasion, I use myself as an example. I do this because I know my stories well and I'm comfortable sharing them with you. I am not suggesting that I'm perfect—far from it, in fact. I'm just offering my experiences, good and bad, for your learning pleasure.

Finally, this book is called *The Proactive Professional*, so the examples I use are primarily related to the working world. However, the lessons are equally applicable in other areas of life. I encourage you to aim for becoming a proactive *person*. Start with your professional life, and the rest will follow.

CHAPTER 3

THE PATH TO MASTERY

BEFORE YOU BEGIN your journey to becoming the proactive professional, I want to help you understand the process of learning a new skill. All too often, I see people get discouraged when they don't experience dramatic improvement *immediately*. They expect mastery to happen within mere moments of picking up a book.

Let's be real. It's taken a lifetime to build your current habits. Breaking them and replacing them with new ones isn't an overnight proposition. And while it's often repeated, the twenty-one-day rule doesn't apply either. In fact, current research shows that the *real* time it takes to break or make a habit is around 66 days on average, though it can range from 18 to 254 (that's nearly a year!).[1]

Actually learning a brand new skill, applying it successfully, and reaping the rewards can take a long time. That's not to say that you won't experience some benefits quickly. You will! A few will almost certainly happen immediately. But true mastery requires sincere, consistent effort on your part.

---

1   Phillippa Lally, "How New Habits Are Formed: Modeling Habit Formation in the Real World," *European Journal of Social Psychology* (July 2009).

To better understand how this works, consider the Stages of Competence, as outlined in figure 1. (Gordon Training International created this model in the 1970s.)

FIGURE 1. THE STAGES OF COMPETENCE

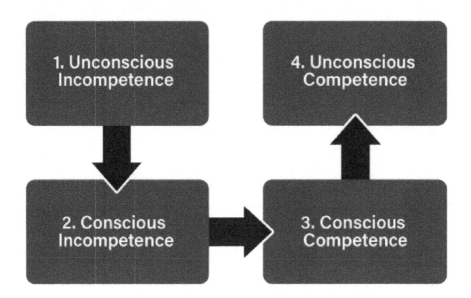

Let's review each stage in detail.

STAGE 1: UNCONSCIOUS INCOMPETENCE

In stage 1, you don't know what you don't know. You're incompetent, but you're not even aware of it. This is how a lot of reactive people live. They might sense that something isn't working, and they most certainly experience some negative consequences, but they can't make the connection to determine what they're doing wrong.

In this stage, you need an outside perspective. You need someone to explain to you what is happening and where your skills are deficient. I was in this stage when my former boss kept telling me to "be proactive." Perhaps someone has told you the same thing. It's an eye-opening experience to have a deficiency spelled out for you like that. It's also a wonderful gift. Otherwise, we'd just continue to stumble around completely unaware of our own incompetence.

STAGE 2: CONSCIOUS INCOMPETENCE

In stage 2, you're aware of your incompetence, but you haven't yet started to change. This is the awkward phase where you know things aren't working and you know why, but you still don't have the tools you need to improve the situation.

It's quite likely that you are currently in stage 2. By virtue of the fact that you're reading this book, I can guess that you know proactivity is an area where you have work to do. Congratulations! You're past the first stage and already on your way to building competence.

In this stage, you need information—real, tangible solutions you can implement. That's a darn good thing too, since that's exactly what this book provides.

STAGE 3: CONSCIOUS COMPETENCE

In stage 3, you put your newfound knowledge to work and experience a state of conscious competence, where you're proficient, but it requires a concerted effort. You really have to think about what you're doing. This isn't a bad thing, but it's exhausting. It's easy to get lazy and lose motivation. When you stop thinking about it, you revert right back to your old habits.

This is the stage where you'll spend the majority of your time as a learner. Here, you need support and patience as you push ahead. Make note of how your efforts are paying off. At first, it may be hard to see. But I assure you, in short order, you *will* see improvement. Don't let those victories inspire you to slack off though! It takes considerable practice to reach the final stage.

STAGE 4: UNCONSCIOUS COMPETENCE

In stage 4, you finally experience unconscious competence—that place where you no longer have to intentionally think about being proactive; you just naturally are. It's ingrained in you. It's how you operate.

Even as a relatively advanced proactive professional, I still bounce back and forth between stage 3 and stage 4. I've been practicing these strategies for years, and sometimes, proactivity feels like it's part of my DNA. I don't even have to try; it just happens. It's instinctively how I think.

Of course, other times, it's more of a challenge. I have to remind myself to rely on my proactive skillset, and sadly, I sometimes revert to reactivity—not because I don't know better, but simply because I get lazy.

Wherever you are, give yourself permission to be there. You can be a work in progress and a masterpiece at the same time. Don't get down on yourself, and don't get lazy. Mastering any skill requires consistent effort over an extended period of time. Make the commitment *now* to see it through.

PART 2

THE PROACTIVE SKILLSET

CHAPTER 4

PROACTIVITY DEFINED

*Destiny is no matter of chance. It's a matter of choice.
It is not a thing to be waited for; it is a thing to be
achieved.*

WILLIAM JENNINGS BRYAN, AMERICAN POLITICIAN (1860–1925)

I HAVE SOME bad news for you…

Your washing machine is about to die. With every load, it sputters and churns, as if gasping its last tortured breath. Yet, for the moment, it still *technically* works.

That's why, when you see a great sale on washing machines at your local home goods store, you hardly take notice. After all, your machine might be dying, but it's not dead yet! There's no point in buying one now when it's not really necessary, right? You've got other, more important things to spend your money on—like your exciting Caribbean vacation!

A few weeks later though, the night before your big vacation, you're rushing to get a few final loads of laundry done when suddenly the machine just stops. The clothes are full of suds, and you spend the evening handwashing your delicates, muttering to yourself that the thing was always a piece of junk.

Once you get back from vacation, all tan and relaxed, you head to the home goods store to pick up a new machine only to find it's now twice the price. The great sale is over, and you have no choice but to fork out the extra cash.

Suddenly, your vacation seems so far away, it's almost like it never happened.

This scenario might sound like a series of unfortunate events, but it was totally predictable and preventable. In this story, you were playing the role of a *reactive* person. Clearly, being reactive can be both frustrating and expensive.

Reactivity is the opposite of proactivity, and it's an easy habit to fall into. It goes hand in hand with procrastination. Why do something today when it's easily put off until tomorrow?

(This is, of course, a rhetorical question. We already know that putting things off until tomorrow creates a bunch of unnecessary pain and anguish.)

Put in the simplest of terms, being proactive means doing the things you need to do *before* you need to do them—like regularly changing the oil in your car instead of waiting for it to start sputtering and spewing smoke. When you're proactive, you keep your car running smoothly and prevent costly repairs. As a result, you experience greater peace of mind and extend the overall lifespan of your vehicle. The minimal investment you make in regularly getting your oil changed pays huge dividends in the long run. That's the essence of proactivity.

Being reactive means you allow circumstances to control you, rather than the other way around. Reactive people only take action when it's absolutely required—when the consequences of inaction are pressing down upon them. It's like waiting to put your seat belt on until you see an accident about to happen or waiting until the day you retire to start saving for retirement. It just doesn't work.

Consider the following example, wherein we meet two individuals we'll get to know well throughout this book, Reactive Rita and Proactive Patty.

Reactive Rita has just been informed that the software she uses to run an important weekly report is being changed. In the next month, a new program will be installed, and all the existing data in the system will migrate over. Rita, like all of us, hates technology changes. But she also knows they're necessary. She bites her tongue and waits for the transition, knowing it's likely to be a nightmare.

Right on schedule, the new software rolls out, and Rita struggles intensely for a few weeks. Her reports are delayed, and the people who rely on them get frustrated. Rita, in turn, gets frustrated herself. After all, it's not her fault! Why are people taking this out on her? The transition is rough, to say the least, but Rita considers herself a victim of circumstances.

Now, let's contrast that with Patty's experience.

Proactive Patty holds the same role as Rita and is also informed of the impending software change. Like Rita, Patty hates technology changes. However, instead of just anxiously waiting like Rita, Patty jumps into action. She empowers herself to take steps to minimize the predictable frustration that accompanies a technology change.

First, she watches a few video tutorials that teach her the basics of the new software. That way, she knows what to expect.

Then, she meets with her colleague in IT to ask him some questions: What are the most important changes she should be aware of? Does he anticipate any challenges in the transition process?

Finally, she calls the people who rely on her weekly reporting to let them know what's happening. That way, if there's a delay, it won't catch them by surprise. They even discuss a few extra steps she can take ahead of time to provide some of the necessary reporting should the data migration go awry.

When the new software rolls out, Patty's learning curve isn't nearly as steep as Rita's. Patty quickly becomes comfortable with the new features and even finds a few efficiencies in the new system. Her reporting is only minimally delayed at first, and no one holds it against her. She's given them ample warning and taken extra steps to ensure their work isn't impacted. In Patty's mind, the technology transition was pretty smooth, all things considered.

See the difference? It's astounding.

Patty took just a few extra steps and created a much better situation for herself and everyone around her. She took control of things she had control over. Sure, she had to deal with the fact that the technology was changing; that part was out of her hands. The only difference between her and Rita was how each of them responded.

Unlike Rita, Patty used her early warning as a launching point for action, and in doing so, she changed the outcome. By proactively preparing for possible problems, Patty actually prevented the problems from occurring at all. Rita, however, ignored the potential problems and thus the likelihood that they would occur actually increased.

Being proactive or reactive isn't just a behavioral characteristic; it's a psychological one as well. Reactive people also allow circumstances to dictate their feelings. When you're stuck in reactivity, your emotional state is at the mercy of outside influences. When you're proactive, you're the one calling the shots.

Rita heard the news and approached the technology transition from a place of disempowerment. As a result, she ended up feeling frustrated and victimized. Patty heard the exact same news and mentally empowered herself. As a result, she felt focused and determined. Their stress levels were entirely different as well. Psychologically, they were at opposite ends of the spectrum from beginning to end.

Given the choice, who would you want to be? The answer is a no-brainer. We all want to be Patty.

Regardless of your position or industry, you can surely relate to the scenario described. We've all experienced the pain of technology changes. But imagine applying these same proactivity principles to the specific challenges you face each and every day.

With the help of this book, you can learn to be proactive in everything you do as a professional. You can proactively manage your tasks and time, so you never again feel like a hamster racing around in a plastic wheel, staying in one place as you run like mad. You can proactively manage your partnerships—with your boss, your colleagues, and even your clients—so you never again find yourself repairing broken relationships. And you can proactively manage your career, so you never again look back and wonder how you ended up here or there.

This isn't to say that you won't still, on occasion, encounter problems in these areas. Being proactive doesn't guarantee a magical life where nothing goes wrong. However, it *does* reduce the number of problems. And it makes those stubborn, unavoidable problems easier to solve because you deal with them early—before they become disasters.

Of course, before you can experience the benefits, you must first understand exactly what's involved in being proactive.

THE PROACTIVE SKILLSET

My first attempt at creating a framework for proactivity came in 2010 and resulted in an article published on my blog.[2] This article outlined something I called the 5P model.

In my continuing studies since then, I've been flattered and disappointed to find that many of the authors exploring this topic reference and rely on 5P as the definitive model for proactivity (and sadly often do so without proper attribution to my work...but that's a personal rant for another day).

---

2 You can find a copy of this article in the appendix.

However, through my continued research, I've come to believe that the 5P model is insufficient. It offers a solid foundation for defining what proactive people do (predict, prevent, plan, participate, and perform), but it fails to explain exactly how it's actually accomplished.

The model presented in this book is far more comprehensive and is the culmination of my ongoing obsession with this topic. It goes beyond the surface level and gets to the heart of how proactive people think and how they do what they do. I have also taught this same model to several corporate clients in a full-day course with great success.

When I tell prospective clients about my course, I'm often met with surprise.

"It takes a whole day to learn one skill?" they ask.

Of course, the time it takes to *teach* something is not the same as the time it takes to actually *learn* it, but I understand their point.

Perhaps you've had similar thoughts about this book: "A whole book devoted to just one skill?"

The reason I can't teach proactivity in a one-hour session or a three-hundred-word blog post is because it's not *one* skill; it's a whole set of skills. And the skills are both behavioral and cognitive.

Confusion around this simple fact is one of the main reasons people struggle to grasp the concept of what it means to be proactive and have trouble truly embracing it in their day-to-day lives.

Proactivity is both an aptitude and an attitude. It's a way of doing and a way of thinking, which, when combined, become a way of being.

It's no wonder that so many smart professionals fail to fully comprehend this multifaceted concept. It's not as simple as you might expect.

If you consider the earlier example featuring our hero, Proactive Patty, you can see hints of the various skills in action. However, if we were to eavesdrop on Patty's mental thought processes, that's where we'd see much of the real behind-the-scenes work.

The Proactive Skillset is made up of six essential elements, which fit together neatly, like the pieces of a puzzle, as illustrated in the figure at the beginning of this chapter. Each piece is necessary, yet each on its own is not enough. Without all the pieces, the picture is incomplete.

Throughout the book, I'll refer to your progression through these six skills as *the proactive journey*. It's an analogy that places you at the center of the action, as a great explorer on a voyage to the future. Each skill will give you the tools you need to make safe passage and bring you closer to your desired destination. References to the proactive journey are noted in parentheses in the following list.

The six skills are as follows:

1. Big Picture Understanding *(Create your map.)*
2. Situational Awareness *(Find your place on the map.)*
3. Future Focus *(Know where you're going.)*
4. Strategic Foresight *(Light your path.)*
5. Intentional Action *(Get moving.)*
6. Self-Evaluation *(Course-correct as needed.)*

In the following chapters, we'll explore each skill in depth. You'll understand exactly what each skill looks like and feels like and why each is necessary for becoming proactive. Most importantly, you'll learn specific steps for developing these skills.

Lastly, it's important to note that, even though the model is presented sequentially, the six skills are, in practice, used simultaneously. The journey, so to speak, is never ending.

But don't worry. All will become clear as you forge ahead.

Yeah, but...

"Being proactive sounds like a lot of extra work."

Really, it's not. Relatively speaking, being proactive requires a small amount of "extra" work on the front end to minimize work on the back end. If done well, your extra work will payoff exponentially, both in reduced workload overall and reduced pain.

If you knew that a few extra steps taken now could prevent problems in the future, why not take them? After all, problems take more time to fix after they become problems, and they're much more frustrating to deal with. Sure, you can't prevent *every* problem from happening. But maybe a few extra steps could reduce the likelihood of them arising or make them easier to fix should they happen in the future.

The worst-case scenario is that yes, you'll waste a little time by trying to be proactive. You can proactively change the oil in your car and still end up with a totally unrelated car problem. But even in that situation, most people would rather know they did what they could.

And sure, maybe your proactive measures won't pay off. After all, if you've been contributing to a 401(k) for decades and, God forbid, you pass away the day before you retire, you never reap the rewards of your proactive effort. But it's still a small price to pay for peace of mind. Perhaps you can even rest a little easier knowing your family will inherit your riches.

⁀

REFLECTION EXERCISES

1. Take some time right now, before you continue reading, and take a good look at the six skills contained in The Proactive Skillset. Based on the little information you have at this point, what do you think they mean? Write your thoughts down, and later, once you've finished reading the book, come back and review what you wrote. You'll be fascinated to see how your understanding evolves.

2. Can you identify a specific time in the recent past when you failed to be proactive and regretted it? What happened, and what were the results? Looking back, what would you have done differently

CHAPTER 5

BIG PICTURE UNDERSTANDING

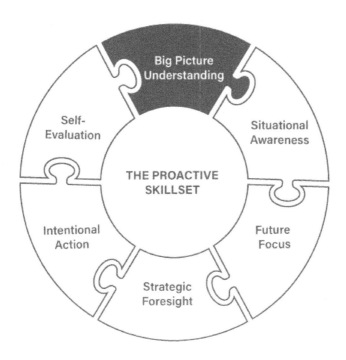

The real voyage of discovery consists not in seeking new landscapes, but in having new eyes.

MARCEL PROUST, FRENCH NOVELIST (1871–1922)

THE FIRST ESSENTIAL component of The Proactive Skillset is Big Picture Understanding. This is defined as *the ability to use broad business acumen to synthesize information and create a holistic view of the professional environment.*

Let's look at that definition in detail. *Broad business acumen* means you possess a base of business knowledge that is both wide and deep. You use that knowledge to *synthesize information*, meaning to process it and create meaning from it. Through that, you *create a holistic*—or complete—*view of the professional environment*, which refers to your unique working world.

Developing this skill is all about gaining perspective. You can't be proactive when you're stuck in your own little bubble. You have to first understand the big picture—all the people, things, situations, and events that are influencing your world. Without that context, you can't effectively exert your own influence.

If you don't appreciate all the things that are impacting your life, you won't ever break free of reactivity. How can you attempt to control your circumstances when you don't have a full and accurate understanding of all the things that contribute to those circumstances? You can't. If you stay focused solely on yourself, the world acts upon you, seemingly without reason, cause, or provocation.

As you set out on the proactive journey, acquiring this first skill is like creating your map. You must shift your gaze outward and examine your surroundings from all points of perspective.

THE POINTS OF PERSPECTIVE

To gain Big Picture Understanding, you must start at the highest point and work your way down. Think of it like going up in an airplane and looking at the world below, just as a mapmaker might. First, you start from a 50,000-foot view, then 40,000 feet, then 30,000 feet, and so on.

FIGURE 2. THE POINTS OF PERSPECTIVE

PERSPECTIVE POINT: THE ECONOMY

The big picture for any professional starts with understanding the economy as a whole. Global, national, regional, and local market conditions and economic trends play an enormous role in our careers and our lives. Yet many people prefer to remain blissfully ignorant. Unfortunately, ignorance does not insulate you.

I've seen too many professionals ignore the trends of the job market, for example, until a sudden layoff puts them smack in the middle of it. I've seen others who couldn't care less about the stock market until they abruptly noticed their retirement accounts were half the size they had been a year ago.

Consider the dire economic forces Millennials were facing when they graduated college in the early part of this century. Many had no idea they were attempting to break into the workforce just as the global economy was beginning to tank. The harsh reality that followed left an entire generation shell-shocked, as vast numbers of educated young people joined the ranks of the unemployed. Now, over a decade later, many continue to struggle with underemployment and slow career progression as a result.

These macroeconomic forces may seem distant and inconsequential, but they are indeed pressing upon us at all times, whether we realize it or not. When we understand them, we're more capable of managing the economic realities of the present and preparing for the economic possibilities of the future. We're able to make smarter, better-informed decisions both personally and professionally.

PERSPECTIVE POINT: YOUR INDUSTRY

As you narrow your perspective, focus next on the industry in which you work.

An *industry* is defined as a group of enterprises that exist within a particular field or businesses that produce similar kinds of products or services.

Industries are like living entities. They experience waves of change—periods of expansion and contraction as new members enter and others fade away. Every industry experiments with innovation while simultaneously perfecting the tried-and-true methods of the past. No viable industry remains stagnant for long.

As a proactive professional, you need to understand what's happening at a macro level so you can operate more effectively at a micro level.

To illustrate my point, allow me to share my own experiences in the mortgage industry. Immediately after college, in 2001, I joined a now-defunct financial institution, which, at the time, was quite well known and reputable. The company was one of the big players in the world of home loans, and as such, my management role involved a heavy amount of sales and origination duties. My paycheck was also directly tied to this aspect of my job.

For those of you who remember, the first decade of the millennium saw a lot of changes in this industry. After September 11, lending rates dropped dramatically. That, coupled with low standards for approval, made it easier than ever for people to get loans. Soon, large numbers of the population were overleveraged, relying solely on home values to support enormous loans and lines of credit, many of which had adjustable interest rates—meaning they could increase after a short period of time. Before long, home prices dropped, rates moved up, payments increased, and that's when the real trouble started.

This is, of course, an oversimplification of one aspect contributing to the United States' credit crisis and great recession. But it serves to explain the volatility of the industry I was in at the time.

Those of us on the inside could see disaster coming, yet, on a macro level, we were powerless to stop it. We had entrusted government and industry leaders with making smart decisions on our behalf—and for the good of the greater economy—but even they seemed at a loss for how to contain the problems headed our way.

On a micro level, all we could do was prepare for the backlash that seemed inevitable. For many, including me, that meant making some tough decisions.

In 2005, I left banking in search of a new career path with a brighter, more stable future. While I remained in financial services for a few more years, working first in credit analysis and then wealth management, I was able to distance myself from the turbulence of the industry.

Three years later, the bank I had worked for was seized by the US government and placed into receivership with the FDIC. Parts of it were acquired at a bargain-basement price, and what was left of the company filed for bankruptcy. To this day, it is considered the largest bank failure in American financial history.

I felt as if I had dodged a bullet by escaping when I did. Millions of people (including some of my former colleagues) lost their jobs, their life savings, and even their homes as a direct result of the failures in this industry. Thankfully, I wasn't one of them.

The people and organizations that remain in the industry today operate under an entirely new set of regulations designed to prevent this sort of thing from happening again. They've had to adapt to a rather dramatic shift in the industry landscape. The ones who have managed to succeed in this tough environment had the foresight to see these changes coming and took proactive steps to prepare.

Having a Big Picture Understanding of your industry gives you the ability to make well-informed choices for yourself and for your career. It helps you prepare for the changes inevitable in any industry, and it provides helpful context for understanding business decisions that may otherwise appear confusing or unexpected.

No organization exists within a vacuum. They're all a part of the greater industry entity and must respond to forces within it. At times, that might mean downsizing or restructuring to remain competitive. It might mean adopting new procedures, acquiring a new technology, or developing a new line of business. When you pay attention to the conditions within your industry, these things not only make sense; they're practically predictable.

PERSPECTIVE POINT: YOUR PROFESSIONAL FIELD

The next point of perspective pertains to your professional field. While an industry is made up of entities all engaged in the same kind of business, a *professional field* is made up of individuals all engaged in the same kind of work.

Like industries, professional fields are constantly evolving in response to changing business needs, technological advancements, and other influences. Consider for example the dramatic changes in the field of office administration within just the past few decades. Gone are the days of typewriters, rotary phones, and ditto machines. The tools of the trade, along with the fundamentals of the job, have been transformed. Today's administrative professionals bear little resemblance to the secretaries of the past.

Your professional field is made up of people who do what you do for a living. They perform your same role, perhaps in other organizations or different industries. Your field may also include those who possess expertise in a shared business function. For example, a recruiter and a benefits coordinator hold different roles but are both broadly included in the field of human resources.

The members of any given field may organize as a collective unit within professional associations. These groups act as leaders for the field by establishing standards and guidelines, providing education, publicizing trends, and more. Some even get involved in the legislative process when new or proposed laws would impact the group.

Gaining Big Picture Understanding requires being connected to others within your field and staying up to date regarding matters that may influence the work you do, whether it's a new regulation, emerging technology, or established best practice. As your field evolves, so must you. That may mean developing a new skill, obtaining a new license or certification, or simply refining your processes in the workplace.

With this knowledge, you can take action early and even stay ahead of the curve in your field. Without it, you have no choice but to be reactive and risk losing your competitive edge.

PERSPECTIVE POINT: YOUR ORGANIZATION

The next point of perspective involves looking at your organization. As a professional, you were hired to fulfill a specific role within the organization you serve. Regardless of what that role is, your ultimate purpose is always to help the organization as a whole to achieve its objectives. Sadly, many professionals have no idea what those objectives actually are or how they're connected to their day-to-day work.

Organizations are complex machines. When you're busy (which is probably most of the time at work), it's both easy and comforting to concentrate on your little corner of this complicated world. But doing so limits your understanding of what you're doing and how it fits into the bigger picture.

Without context, you risk losing sight of your true purpose. You spend more time reacting to immediate, short-term needs rather than proactively addressing the things that really contribute value.

In many organizations, objectives and priorities also tend to shift frequently. If you do not stay attuned to these changes, you can easily end up focusing on the wrong things, wasting precious time, energy, and other resources. With more information, you can proactively participate and intelligently adjust to such changes, rather than mindlessly react.

In order to possess a Big Picture Understanding at this level, you need to first understand the goals of your organization and how those goals are filtered down and distributed to the various divisions and departments within it. Beyond that, you need to understand how the various roles within the organization, including your own, contribute to fulfilling those objectives.

Obviously, you can't expect to be in the know regarding *everything* that's happening within your organization. That wouldn't be practical, and it's unnecessary. But you should make efforts to remain reasonably informed and consider the implications of what you learn. With this context, you're able to be much more strategic in your own role and as a member of the larger team.

To illustrate this point, consider the following scenario.

> Patty is put in charge of a project that will require the assistance of a number of individuals from across her organization. One of those people is Claire, a senior graphic designer from the marketing department.
>
> A week into Patty's project, the organization announces a massive rebranding effort scheduled to begin in the next month. When Patty gets word of this, she connects with Claire to learn more about how this may impact the designer's availability for the project. As it turns out, Claire is predicting she'll be heavily involved in the new rebranding effort and her time will, in fact, be very limited as of next month. But she's happy to help in the meantime.

Patty, proactive as ever, uses this Big Picture Understanding to adjust her project plan and shift the majority of Claire's work to the front end, taking advantage of her availability for the next few weeks. She also coordinates with Claire to determine who can contribute to the project in her absence later once the rebranding initiative really kicks into gear.

Meanwhile, Reactive Rita, Patty's counterpart, is so focused on her own project and her own needs that the news of the rebranding effort doesn't even faze her. Claire, consumed with her own work, doesn't think to mention it. Of course, once the rebranding initiative begins, Rita gets frustrated with Claire's lack of availability and is left scrambling to adjust her plans on the fly.

Once again, Rita is stuck playing catch up while Patty remains two steps ahead.

Having a Big Picture Understanding at this level helps direct your efforts toward the right activities, even when organizational objectives are moving targets.

PERSPECTIVE POINT: YOUR TEAM

The next point of perspective is to look at your *team*, the group of people with whom you work cooperatively to accomplish a shared set of goals.

High-functioning teams create *synergy*, where the whole is actually greater than the sum of its parts. With synergy, the team works more effectively than the same group of individuals would if left to work on their own.

Synergy, like proactivity, is only made possible with perspective. It requires that each team member understand his or her own role and contributions but also that each recognizes and appreciates the distinct roles and contributions of others. With this knowledge, the team can work together as a cohesive group, leveraging each individual's strengths and expertise while filling in the gaps for one another when needed.

As a proactive professional, this kind of Big Picture Understanding allows you to allocate resources more effectively and contribute more value to the team. When you're planning a vacation, for example, you can make intelligent recommendations regarding how your workload might be distributed among team members in your absence. When working collaboratively with the team, you can pre-empt problems by considering what others are working with in terms of information, time, and other possible limitations. You can address their needs early on and thus facilitate greater levels of synergy.

Once again, it's neither practical nor necessary to understand *every* detail regarding what's happening on your team. Do your best to remain reasonably informed and use what you learn to build a more complete picture of your day-to-day work environment.

POINT OF PERSPECTIVE: YOU

This final perspective point should be an easy one. Most people naturally look at the world from a somewhat self-centered point of view—*I am the star of my own movie!*

While focusing solely on this perspective is indeed dangerous, it does provide an important piece of the full picture. Without it, we fail to understand our part in creating our own experiences.

All of these other factors certainly influence our big picture, but we are still a key player in the show. Our world is the result of a great many things, including our own abilities, beliefs, values, choices, and actions. *Being proactive means recognizing the outside factors at play while also taking responsibility for that which we create.*

At this level, you look at yourself—your own strengths and weaknesses, your roles and responsibilities, your power and limitations. From this perspective, we gain an appreciation of our personal contributions to the big picture. We see our own influence on our own world.

Reactive people struggle with this. It's easier to look outward, at the many external factors shaping your world and to see yourself as a victim of circumstance, rather than a part of it. But you are, indeed, an essential part of this world in which you exist. Who you are and what you do are critical elements of the story.

Certainly you don't control the powerful forces that surround you. Nor do they have the ability to control you. They merely influence your experiences, just as you influence the outcome. You have the ability to use the resources at your disposal to respond to these forces in any way you choose.

As you progress through the proactive journey, you'll learn more about how to use your influence to create the outcomes you want. For now, your job is simply to recognize that you *do* have a very important part to play in the big picture.

USING THE POINTS OF PERSPECTIVE

You'll notice that figure 2, which I've used to illustrate this concept, is an inverted pyramid. It shows *you* at the bottom with the five points of perspective organized in three distinct layers above.

The economy is at the highest and widest point and is a single layer unto itself. This is because it represents the most expansive force in our professional world; its influence trickles down and touches all of the areas beneath it.

Your industry and *your professional field* both appear in the middle layer. This is because these items both represent the competitive environment.

Their influence trickles down and touches the bottom layer—*your team* and *your organization*—both of which represent the collaborative environment.

Note, however, that this doesn't mean competition and collaboration are exclusive to these areas. You likely experience some level of competition within your organization and your team. Likewise, collaboration may exist within your industry and your professional field. Labeling the second layer as "competitive" and layer 3 as "collaborative" acknowledges only the most basic nature of these forces.

You appear at the very bottom tip of the pyramid because all of these forces are working simultaneously above you, filtering down to shape your professional world. However, you are an equally powerful force.

Exploring the points of perspective helps you build your map. As you do so, look for connections. Ask yourself how what's happening in one area impacts the landscape of the others. These are not distinct and separate entities. They are merely different layers of the same big picture.

HOW TO DEVELOP BIG PICTURE UNDERSTANDING

Developing Big Picture Understanding means understanding your environment. It requires taking responsibility for your part and taking an active role in creating your map.

Becoming an enthusiastic and tireless consumer of information is an essential step in this process. However, in order to synthesize the information you consume, you must also have a strong foundation of business knowledge—that's what makes it possible to see connections and apply real-world meaning to what you learn.

The following strategies will help you accomplish both sides of this skill.

READ, READ, AND READ SOME MORE

It should come as no surprise that Big Picture Understanding is a natural by-product of being a voracious reader. If you wouldn't currently describe yourself as such, it's time to develop the habit.

And it is, indeed, a habit that takes concerted effort and a commitment of time. Unfortunately, information can't be acquired through osmosis. Believe me, I've tried. In fact, in my teen years, I distinctly remember buying a set of tarot cards along with a book that explained how to use them. I immediately shoved the book onto a shelf, opened the cards, and started reading fortunes for all my friends. They very quickly lost interest when it became clear that I was a fraud.

A bookshelf full of good intentions might make a nice impression on guests, but it's not worth the dust it collects. The value is in the reading.

Of course, these days, time and energy are not the only obstacles to overcome in developing the habit of reading. In our modern world, we have a massive amount of information available at our fingertips, and it's a double-edged sword in some respects. With such easy access to information, how do you know where to focus your attention? How do you separate the golden nuggets of valuable, credible information from the torrent of useless, unreliable junk that surrounds it?

You must become a *discerning* consumer—one who seeks accurate and timely information from a wide variety of high-quality sources and trusted experts. Use your best judgment and consider the following:

- Is the information presented based on fact and evidence, or is it someone's interpretation of fact and evidence? Both can be valuable, but you don't want to mistake one for the other.
- Is the author reputable in this field of study? What affiliations or biases may be influencing the information presented? Does there

appear to be a motive not related to education? (For example, is there a motive to sell something or influence voters?)

- Does the information align with what you already know, and does it pass the common sense test? If you're reading something that forces you to make great leaps in logic or contradicts your existing knowledge, seek additional sources before buying in.
- When was this written? Is the information likely to change over time? Is it possible that new information would materially change what is presented? If so, seek newer sources.

What you read matters, so be a thoughtful consumer.

At this point, you may be wondering how much reading is required to consider yourself a voracious reader and gain Big Picture Understanding. Here are some general recommendations by category.

READ SIX BUSINESS-RELATED BOOKS PER YEAR (MINIMUM).

Books offer an in-depth exploration of topics, making them ideal for building business acumen. I earned a business degree in college, so when I entered the workforce, I had a base level of business knowledge. I spoke the language, you might say. I wasn't fluent by any means, but the concepts weren't entirely foreign.

That's what reading can do for you. It helps you get familiar with an idea, and then, as you apply what you've learned in the real world, you gain deeper understanding. Whether or not you've ever studied business formally, you have the ability to study it on your own with the help of books. No matter what your level of education is, there's always more to learn, and there's no shortage of great books available to help.

Six books per year equates to one every two months—a reasonable, achievable goal for most professionals. (And yes, this book counts as one for this year!)

Choose books related to topics that pique your interest: communication, technology, leadership, productivity, organizational change and improvement, strategic management, or anything else related to the business world.

To help you get started, I've included a list of some of my favorite books under the heading "Reading Recommendations" in the appendix.

READ ONE PUBLICATION FOR YOUR FIELD OR INDUSTRY PER MONTH.

Most professional associations and industry (trade) groups offer a variety of materials to disseminate relevant information to their members. This may include items such as the following:

- magazines or newsletters
- trend/research reports
- white papers and case studies

These materials generally contain news regarding issues facing the group and perspectives on how to address these challenges.

While some materials are only made available to paying group members, other items are also available to the public. I highly recommend becoming a member of an active group that is relevant to your career. However, if it's cost prohibitive, don't let that stop you from seeking information. Take advantage of what you can for free.

Reading one publication a month in this category is not difficult to do when you know where to look. *Wikipedia* has a comprehensive list of professional associations in the United States, which, at the time of this writing, contains 422 individual groups. Any group worth your time will have a website, and most will be full of useful reading. This is a great place to start.

READ LOCAL, NATIONAL, AND GLOBAL NEWS PUBLICATIONS EACH WEEK.

We've already established that the economy is a key point of perspective for Big Picture Understanding. It represents the highest point in our model, meaning its influence trickles down and affects all the elements beneath it. However, in reality, there are even higher points of perspective not shown in our model—forces that trickle down and influence the economy itself.

In order to understand what's happening in the economy, you need at least some understanding of these higher-level influences as well. Current events, market conditions, business matters, and politics all play a role in the state of the economy on a local, national, and global level.

Some of my favorite publications in this category include the following:

- *Fast Company* (www.FastCompany.com)
- *Forbes* (www.Forbes.com)
- *Inc. Magazine* (www.Inc.com)
- *Newsweek* (www.newsweek.com)
- The *Wall Street Journal* (www.wsj.com)
- *USA Today* (www.USAToday.com)

These publications specialize in national and global news and business-related matters. You may also want to find a few local and regional publications to get a well-rounded perspective.

For many, myself included, reading "the news" is a delicate balancing act. Remember that bad news sells, sensational headlines capture attention, and instilling fear keeps readers coming back. There's an endless stream of this stuff.

Those who invest too much time or emotional energy may find themselves feeling helpless, frustrated, and anxious. Finding your right balance is like the Goldilocks test—only you can determine what's too much, too little, or just right.

What has worked best for me, particularly in the past few years, is to simply skim my favorite news sources one to three times per week. This keeps me broadly informed but prevents saturation and the inevitable emotional turmoil that follows. I'm aware of what's happening in the world and the economy without being consumed by the drama of it.

READ ANY MATERIAL PRODUCED FOR, BY, OR ABOUT YOUR ORGANIZATION.

This recommendation is a tall order, I realize. While it may not be possible to read *everything* in this category, make it your goal. After all, if your organization deems information worthy of sharing, or if others deem information *about* your organization worthy of sharing, it's almost certainly worthy of your attention.

Items in this category may include:

- PR and marketing material, such as the organization's website and press releases
- public financial reports
- company newsletters (internal and external) and announcements
- articles about your organization published on the web, in business journals, or by news outlets (hint: set up a Google alert to notify you)

ENGAGE IN TRAINING ACTIVITIES

Reading, of course, is not the only way to consume information. Sometimes, it's not even the best way. Particularly when you're trying to understand complicated and advanced business topics, it's often more effective to participate in training activities.

Training is ideal for building broad business acumen, and there are many options available. Virtual training, conducted via webinar or videoconference, is convenient and cost-effective because it doesn't require travel. In-person training typically takes place at conferences, seminars, and other professional events. While you're there, you'll also get to interact with colleagues in your field as well as professionals from other fields, so in-person training events are a great way to expand your perspective even further.

Generally, I recommend that all professionals spend about thirty to forty hours per year devoted to professional development training activities. This can be achieved by attending a weeklong conference for your profession, for example, or one all-day seminar per quarter, or a variety of smaller educational sessions throughout the year.

Once again, professional associations and industry (trade) groups are helpful resources for learning about relevant training opportunities. Trusted experts and leaders in your field may also offer public training sessions on topics of interest. Lastly, established training companies (such as Fred Pryor Seminars) also offer plenty of options throughout the country. However, while many of these programs are quite informative, your training experience often depends on the quality of the instructor. Full disclosure: I'm a former Fred Pryor instructor myself, and I had quite an eclectic variety of colleagues.

ASK QUESTIONS

People are often the best sources we have for information. Everyone we encounter has a unique perspective that can help create a more complete view of the big picture. Simply by asking the right questions, we can gain valuable insight.

Early on in my career, I thought asking questions of others would only show my ignorance. Over time, I discovered that thoughtful questions actually demonstrate intelligence, curiosity, and engagement. I also learned that most people are quite eager to share their thoughts, experience, and wisdom with someone who is genuinely interested.

Ask your colleagues what they're working on to learn more about your team. Ask people from other departments what their top priorities are to better understand your organization. Ask your manager how certain events might impact your industry or how industry changes might impact your organization. Ask people in your field what trends they're seeing or how they envision the field might change over the next five years.

Remember that these questions aren't meant to feel like an interrogation. You want your tone to say, "I'm genuinely interested in hearing your perspective on this," not, "I'm just being nosy." Also, be respectful of time. People are busy and such conversations are generally considered a luxury.

However, asking questions is *particularly* important when something directly impacts you or your work but you don't have enough context to truly make sense of it.

A participant in one of my training sessions (we'll call him Mark) experienced this early in his career. As a junior financial analyst, Mark was responsible for creating a comprehensive weekly report. For the first few months in his role, Mark diligently pulled data from a variety of sources, organized it in the pre-established format, and delivered the final report to his boss. Frequently, the boss would request changes, and Mark would quickly jump to accommodate. The process was time consuming to say the least. But over time, it also grew frustrating.

The problem? Mark had no idea what this report was actually used for. He knew it was a key responsibility for his job, but he didn't understand why. To him, the report appeared useless.

Thankfully, Mark was a naturally proactive person. His intuition told him he was lacking Big Picture Understanding and without that, he would forever remain stuck in reactivity.

In order to gain some clarity, Mark initiated a conversation with his boss. He asked specific questions: What is the data used for? Who sees the report? What purpose does it serve?

The answers he received were enlightening.

With his new Big Picture Understanding, Mark was able to make helpful improvements to the reporting process. He found ways to make the report even more useful, and the number of change requests decreased dramatically. He no longer resented the time-consuming task because he understood its importance.

Mark was able to become an active participant in the process, where before, he merely performed as directed. He was able to add real value, and it all started with asking a few questions and gaining Big Picture Understanding.

Yeah, but...

"I don't have the time or money for all this reading and training you recommend."

Let's talk about reading first.

I'll make you a promise right now: all of my reading recommendations can be achieved in just thirty minutes a day. Over a year, that equals more than 180 hours of reading.

Personally, I prefer paper, but e-books are an option. Public libraries actually carry both, and online booksellers like

Amazon have an enormous, ever-changing selection of free e-books. As of this writing, there are over ten thousand free e-books from Amazon in the self-improvement category. Even if you don't have an e-reader, you can read them on *any* device by downloading a free app, like the Amazon Kindle app.

I'm also a huge fan of audiobooks and podcasts for those of us who like to learn while commuting, working out, cleaning the house, or walking the dog. Bonus—a good audiobook always motivates me to spend a few extra minutes on the treadmill!

Finally, some online publishers will aggregate relevant materials into a single digest or e-newsletter and deliver it via email on a weekly or monthly basis, saving you the time it takes to search for individual items on your own. Social media tools, such as Twitter, Facebook, and LinkedIn, can also act as aggregators. Many trusted experts and business leaders in various fields frequently share high-quality, free reading material with their followers. Connect with these people, and while you're there, search for your preferred publications as well. Many have active social media profiles, which can help you quickly and easily identify items you'd like to add to your reading list.

Now, let's talk about training, shall we?

High-quality training does, indeed, cost money. But there are some wonderful free training resources available as well. Ted Talks, for example, are short (twenty minutes or less), inspiring, educational presentations done by some of the world's most influential thought leaders. There are currently over two thousand Ted Talks videos available on **www.Ted.com** for free.

Free training webinars are also widely available online. If you keep your eye out, you may even find some free in-person training opportunities in your area. However, "free" often means you'll get a sales pitch along the way. So be prepared and keep your expectations in check.

In my opinion, and as someone who makes a living in the training industry, it's worthwhile to pay for high-quality training activities. A paid training experience is typically a much better use of your time because everything is designed to deliver educational value. The training isn't merely a marketing tool; it's a paid service. Always do your due diligence first, however, as some are more deserving of your money than others.

How much should you plan to spend on professional development training? For this question, I always refer to Brian Tracy, a longtime leader in the field of self-improvement, who suggests 3 percent of gross income is a practical goal. That means if you earn $50,000 annually, you should spend about $1,500 per year on your own development.

Brian Tracy also makes an intriguing promise. He says that for every one dollar you invest in your own growth, you'll increase your personal bottom line by thirty dollars. That's an amazing return on investment! But let me also offer my own words of caution: this return might not be *immediately* evident. But remember that, as you build your business acumen, as you develop Big Picture Understanding, and as you explore the points of perspective, you will be making yourself a more marketable asset in the professional world. Your value within your own organization will increase and over time, so will your earning potential. Investing in yourself is indeed a proactive choice.

IN SUMMARY

Big Picture Understanding is the foundation upon which the entire proactive skillset is built. It's the first step in the proactive journey.

The recommendations in this chapter are not intended to be an exhaustive list of activities for building Big Picture Understanding. There are, of course, other things you can do to increase your understanding of the many influences that shape your professional world. The only requirement is that you keep your eyes and ears open and foster a spirit of *insatiable curiosity*.

The map you are creating will guide you on the rest of your journey. Without a complete and accurate map, you're doomed to stay in the same place or, worse, to wander aimlessly for eternity.

It's also important to realize that this process is ongoing. Do not chisel your map in stone. Remember that the details can change at any time. Allow new information to reshape your view of the environment and revise your map as needed so it's always up to date.

The next skill will help you do that and so much more.

REFLECTION EXERCISES

1. Rate your overall current level of Big Picture Understanding on a scale of one to ten, where one is "wildly insufficient" and ten is "expert." Then, break down your overall rating by assessing each individual perspective point using the same scale. Which one(s) need the most work, and what specifically will you do to gain deeper understanding?

2. Make a list of your favorite resources for expanding your Big Picture Understanding, including authors and experts; websites and other reading materials; groups and specific individuals; and anything else that applies. Share your list with trusted colleagues and ask them to expand on it by sharing their favorites. Keep your list handy and rely on these resources when you're especially concerned with getting the most out of your limited time. Explore and find new resources to add to your list when you have the time or need.

CHAPTER 6

SITUATIONAL AWARENESS

In rivers, the water that you touch is the last of what has passed and the first of that which comes; so with present time.

Leonardo da Vinci, Italian polymath (1452–1519)

THE SECOND ESSENTIAL component of The Proactive Skillset is Situational Awareness. This is defined as *the ability to observe and interpret immediate surroundings to enhance understanding of present circumstances.*

If developing Big Picture Understanding is like building a mental map of your professional world, this next skill is like sticking a big red "You Are Here" pin in that map. It's the skill of knowing where you are at any given moment and staying attuned to the changing landscape that surrounds you. Your Big Picture Understanding is what helps you own it and make sense of it.

Looking at the definition more closely, we see that Situational Awareness involves a number of steps. First, we must *observe*, or notice, what is happening in our *immediate surroundings*. We also must *interpret* that information, which means we filter it through our lens of understanding to create meaning. The reason we do this is to *enhance our understanding of present circumstances* so we're always aware of the current reality in which we're operating.

Situational Awareness is a term frequently used in the world of security and self-defense. We're warned that the best way to protect ourselves is to stay aware of our surroundings—take note when people are behaving strangely or when something around you just doesn't feel right. In short, to put yourself in the best position for safety, you must stay mindful of what's happening around you.

In terms of proactivity, Situational Awareness is what helps us operate within a dynamic environment where things are continuously changing. After all, we can't proactively plan and prepare for the future if we don't first accurately understand our present. It's easy to take our circumstances for granted and to assume we know what's happening without ever really looking. Further, when our circumstances change, we often continue to see things as they *should* be rather than as they actually are. As a result, we remain stuck in reactivity. Situational Awareness helps us see reality as it is—an essential building block for becoming proactive.

THE PARADOX OF PATTERNS

One of the most common reasons our Situational Awareness fails us is due to something I call the *paradox of patterns*.

A *paradox* is when a situation has elements that are contradictory. Patterns, or routines, are indeed a paradox because they are both helpful and unhelpful when it comes to proactivity.

A *pattern* is a pre-established way of doing things. For example, imagine a pattern that a seamstress follows to create a dress. A pattern is also repeatable. That seamstress can make that same dress over and over again using the same pattern. She knows exactly how it will turn out every time, and after a while, it's practically effortless to make.

In the workplace, patterns are helpful because they provide insight regarding what to expect—something we'll discuss much more in chapter 8.

Interestingly, when we're operating within a known pattern, we tend to mentally disengage. We go on autopilot, just like the seamstress. In many ways, this is helpful because we reserve our mental energy for tasks that might need it more. After all, we don't want to consume a heavy amount of mental energy on *every* step of *every* task—that would be exhausting. When we're doing something we've done a million times before, we want to rely on the pattern and give our brains a rest.

However, this can also create problems. If we're not careful, patterns can lull us into a sense of complacency and blind us to reality.

When something is familiar, we begin to miss important signals that conditions have somehow changed. We simply act based on the expected pattern until suddenly we realize we're off track. We're like the seamstress, continuing to make that exact same dress, even when her client has asked for a coat.

Situational Awareness breaks us out of mindless rhythm. It helps ensure we always know our place on an ever-changing map.

LEVELS OF AWARENESS

It's important to clarify exactly what kind of awareness we're talking about here. Let's look at four different levels.

FIGURE 3. LEVELS OF AWARENESS

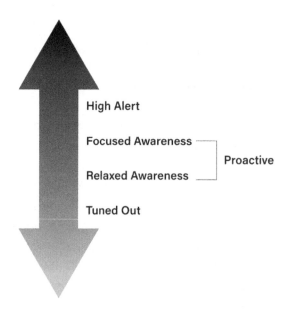

High Alert

Focused Awareness

Relaxed Awareness

Proactive

Tuned Out

LEVEL 1: TUNED OUT

At this level, you're not paying attention to your surroundings; you're simply going through the motions. If you've ever arrived at the front door of your home only to realize you can't remember the drive you took to get there, you know what it's like to be tuned out. In this state, you're physically present, but you're not mentally present.

You can even do fairly complex tasks—like driving—while in this mental fog, though your ability to perform well is certainly hampered.

Most of us have experienced this before, and, admittedly, it's a little scary. Being tuned out isn't a safe or responsible way of maneuvering through life, whether on the road or in the workplace.

LEVEL 2: RELAXED AWARENESS

In this state, you're attentive, yet comfortable. This is how we drive on our best behavior. We notice the car impatiently merging into our lane, and we smoothly adjust to make room. We do our best to avoid danger and not to cause it.

Relaxed awareness means your demeanor is composed, your focus open. You're taking information in and processing it calmly. It's a pleasant experience for the most part and not too mentally taxing. This is the ideal state both in the workplace and on the road.

LEVEL 3: FOCUSED AWARENESS

This third level is a much more heightened state of awareness; it's like driving in a snowstorm. Your concentration is intensely focused. You've got two hands on the wheel and eyes straight ahead. No messing around with the radio or talking on your cell phone. It's all business.

In this state, it's easy to become so engrossed in one area of concern (the icy road, for example) that you're more likely to miss other details (say, an approaching detour sign). While focused awareness is necessary in certain conditions, spending too much time in this state is both stressful and exhausting.

LEVEL 4: HIGH ALERT

The fourth and final level is that of high alert—the adrenaline-fueled, impulsive response to an immediate threat. It's what happens in that split-second when you realize the car in your peripheral vision isn't going to stop for the red light. Your body and mind reflexively kick into high alert as you run through the options before you at lightning speed.

Typically, in the high alert state, focus narrows dramatically as you deal with the impending danger that's right in front of you. The sense of panic that accompanies it, however, can hamper judgment and lead to questionable decision making. Spending too much time in high alert can leave you feeling frantic and frazzled.

THE LEVELS OF AWARENESS IN ACTION

Collectively, as a species, our Situational Awareness skills have been on the decline for many, many years. While our cave dwelling ancestors obviously didn't use these skills on the road, they were naturally more aware of their surroundings. After all, in those days, if you didn't pay attention, you were likely to end up facing down a bear or meeting some other deadly fate.

In our modern era, few of us face such life-threatening dangers on a daily basis. Instead, the *dangers* we're likely to encounter in today's workplace threaten our job security, our ability to perform at peak levels, and our professional reputation. In their own way, such threats are equally important to our survival and worthy of our attention.

Unlike our ancestors, we also have a record number of distractions vying for our attention. Our awareness is already stretched thin. Throw in a few comfortable patterns, and it's no surprise that so many professionals have incredibly poor Situational Awareness skills.

Reactive people tend to vacillate between level 1 and level 4 awareness. For many, this is the result of a vicious cycle. Reactive people spend a lot of time tuned out. They are victims of their own patterns, mindlessly doing what they've always done without bothering to look around and make sure it's still the *right* thing. They are the oblivious driver, barreling down the road, ignoring everyone else and disregarding the signs of dangerous conditions ahead.

Inevitably, reactive people are jolted into a state of high alert when the danger is immediately upon them. In that moment, they're forced to react, and it's usually in a very haphazard kind of way. Once the situation appears reasonably resolved, however, reactive people are quick to tune out once again. And thus the cycle continues.

Proactive people spend most of their time in level 2 awareness. They're comfortably engaged; they use patterns intelligently and don't let them drag their awareness down to level 1. They know when to flex to level 3 but also recognize when conditions have improved and it's time to ease back to level 2. For proactive people, level 4 (high alert) is very uncommon because few things catch them off guard.

Let's check back in with our friends, Proactive Patty and Reactive Rita, to see these principles in action.

> Both Patty and Rita are managing important, long-term projects at their organization. Once a month, they each conduct a short progress report presentation for the executive leadership board. In the past, these presentations have always been quick and casual.
>
> However, this month, several concerns have arisen regarding the two projects. Budgets are running dangerously high, timelines have been drastically altered, and technology troubles are

plaguing the team. Rumors are circulating that both projects are off course and headed for disaster.

Thanks to her state of relaxed awareness (level 2), Proactive Patty knows exactly what is happening in all areas of her project. She also knows that this month's presentation to the board is critical; she wants to ease their fears and assure them she's still the right person for this role.

With this in mind, Patty decides to change her approach for the presentation. Instead of the usual informal update, she prepares a thorough report. In it, she outlines the challenges facing the project, why they exist, what she's done to address them, and how she plans to continue addressing them in the future.

When she enters the boardroom, Patty shifts into a pure state of focused awareness (level 3). She offers her full attention to the group, acknowledging their concerns and confronting the issues head-on. She answers their questions before they even think to ask. As she concludes, Patty reiterates her passion for the project's big picture purpose and her determination to see it through to successful completion.

Rita, on the other hand, doesn't have the same keen sense of Situational Awareness. Because she's mostly tuned out (level 1), she's actually surprised to hear so many questions and concerns raised during her presentation. In the past, these things were always so laid back. She hasn't prepared any more than usual, and that quickly proves to be a mistake.

Once she realizes what she's up against, Rita shifts into high alert (level 4). She's now hyperaware of the scrutiny she's facing and scrambles to come up with answers. In her ill-prepared state, her vague responses sound out of touch and defensive. The executives are left wondering if Rita really has what it takes to see this project through.

DEVELOPING SITUATIONAL AWARENESS

At this point, we've established that, as a proactive professional, your goal is to spend most of your time in level 2 awareness, flexing to level 3 when needed. Ideally, you want to stay out of level 1 and level 4. Now, let's explore how to do that.

PRACTICE WHOLE-SELF OBSERVATION

The key to Situational Awareness is whole-self observation—the ability to see, hear, and even feel what's happening around you and within you. It's a process that requires all five senses, an engaged mind, and an intuitive heart. In short, whole-self observation is a physical, mental, and emotional exercise.

Whole-self observation is about studying both content and conditions. *Content* has to do with substance—what is happening or what is being said—while *conditions* have to do with everything else—how people are feeling and acting and the overall atmosphere.

To practice this kind of observation, you must search for the real meaning beneath the surface of things. *Truth reveals itself if you invest your whole self in finding it.*

You must pay attention to what others are communicating—not just with their words but their tone of voice, facial expressions, body language, and actions. You must listen for what is said as well as what is not said. You must also consider the other information at your disposal—your Big Picture Understanding, your experience, and even your gut instinct.

With knowledge of both content and conditions, you can draw more accurate conclusions regarding meaning and thus, in theory, make better decisions and take more effective action in response.

In our earlier example, the *content* was the same for both Proactive Patty and Reactive Rita—they were both expected to conduct a presentation to the executive board regarding the progress of their projects. That's what was happening. In the past, the presentation had been a relatively informal affair, but *conditions* had changed. The projects were experiencing challenges.

Patty, using her whole-self observation skills, was aware of the concerns and understood what they meant. She knew the executives would be anxious. She knew they'd have questions, and she needed to have answers.

Rita, on the other hand, fell victim to the pattern. She either wasn't aware of the new conditions or didn't understand what they meant. Reactive people tend to overlook conditions until faced directly with the consequences.

Whole-self observation helps us tune in to critical, though often hidden, information. It is both an external process and an internal one. It's not enough to focus solely on outward circumstances. You must also turn your observation inward. Monitor your own physical, mental, and emotional presence. What are *you* experiencing, and what role does that play in your situation?

Feeling tired and stressed? Maybe it's not the best time to broach that difficult conversation with a coworker. Feeling focused and energized? Maybe it's time to tackle that complicated task you've been dreading.

Of course, you can't always let your conditions dictate your content. Sometimes, you'll find yourself having that difficult conversation when tired and stressed. Sometimes, because of external pressures, you'll be forced to work on that complicated task even when your head just isn't in the game. Whole-self observation is essential in these moments too. Monitor your conditions in the process and take an active role in managing them if needed. Don't allow yourself to slip into reactivity by disengaging your awareness.

It's worthwhile noting that humans also have an amazing ability to subconsciously detect details within themselves and their environment. Often, this is translated into an indistinct "gut feeling." Take note of such things and dissect them carefully. They frequently carry valuable messages if you're paying attention.

SHARPEN CRITICAL THINKING SKILLS

We aren't developing Situational Awareness to be intrusive or nosy. We're doing it to better understand our present circumstances. With more information, we can make better decisions and take more effective action.

Obviously, we don't have the capacity or capability to ever truly know *every* single detail of what's happening in any given moment. Instead, we must prioritize our observations and consciously choose where to put our awareness. Not everything is important.

The $6 million question is: How do we know what's worth our attention and what's not?

The answer is simple: Our critical thinking skills guide us in determining what has significance and in deciphering what that significance actually is. Critical thinking skills enable us to connect the dots between what we observe and what it means.

Thinking critically means we analyze what we observe and first ask, "Is it relevant?" If not, we disregard it.

For our purposes, I'll suggest that something is relevant when it impacts you (or your work) or has the ability to do so in the future. This definition keeps our focus considerably broad while also limiting it, which is the goal. Admittedly, this definition is not adequate in all situations, and some readers may morally object to it. However, I encourage you to adopt this perspective for the purpose of this discussion and then later re-evaluate what *relevant* means for you.

A quick example: If I know my coworker is under intense pressure because of an approaching deadline, I would consider that relevant. It might impact how I interact with her or the expectations I have of her with regard to other, lower priority tasks. In short, I'll give her some space to focus on the big deadline. *What* she is working on, however, isn't necessarily relevant. If it's not a project I'm involved with or will be involved with, it's none of my concern. I don't need to waste attention on it.

When observations *are* relevant, we must then take our analysis a step further and ask, "*How* is it relevant?"

To understand the relevance of an observation, you must reflect on it and process it through the lens of what you already know. For this, you'll rely on two critical factors: your Big Picture Understanding and your experience. These things, combined with logic and sound judgment, will help you turn observations into meaningful, useful information.

KEEP CALM

Situational Awareness is greatly hindered by stress and agitation. These things dramatically degrade your ability to focus over any significant amount of time. Likewise, they often lead to fatigue, which can greatly increase the likelihood of tuning out or falling victim to the comfortable rhythm of an established pattern.

Staying calm improves your ability to observe the world around you clearly and accurately and over a sustained period of time.

In many ways, being calm and being proactive are like the chicken and the egg—no one knows which comes first. In order to be proactive, you must remain calm. However, remaining calm is much easier when you're proactive. Regardless of which truly comes first—and regardless of where you are in your proactive journey—adopting a calm demeanor is a useful tool.

In the aviation industry, Situational Awareness is a frequent topic of study for obvious reasons. It's no surprise that many experienced pilots, including my father, are quite stoic. They are taught to remain calm, even under intense pressure. In doing so, they are better equipped to absorb and interpret large amounts of critical information and respond intelligently.

In recent years, an old motivational poster with the words "Keep Calm and Carry On" gained renewed popularity. Originally produced by the British government in 1939 to raise morale in preparation for World War II, the words still ring true many decades later. These days, "Keep Calm and..." posters are a pop culture phenomenon featuring thousands of variations on the theme.

Our poster would read, "Keep Calm and Pay Attention." This is the essence of level 2 awareness. It's a simple concept that is difficult in execution. It requires mental, physical, and emotional grace.

There is no shortage of stress management advice available. Much of it offers tips that, again, sound simplistic ("Remember to breathe!" is a popular one). But even the most basic necessities are often forgotten when you are agitated and under stress. These kinds of reminders can help bring you back into self-awareness.

If this is an area of struggle for you, devote a little time and energy to improving it.

KNOW WHAT YOU DON'T KNOW

Understand that Situational Awareness only goes so far. There will always be things you don't know and can't reasonably expect to know about your surrounding environment and circumstances. We run into trouble when we start to believe our understanding of a situation is complete and 100 percent accurate. Much of the time, there is a lot we don't know, and that's perfectly OK, provided we know that.

No matter how fine-tuned our Situational Awareness is, we must allow for the fact that others may still hold important pieces of the puzzle that we don't have. The best we can do is gather what's available. We must make intelligent guesses and logical leaps based on the information at our disposal, without necessarily assuming we're irrefutably correct.

If a policy change is instituted, for example, we may know the new procedure, and we may *think* we know why the change was needed. However, it would be dangerous to circumvent the new policy and create our own procedure in its place—even if it achieved the same end. Our understanding of the reason behind the policy change is only an educated guess. There are too many unknown factors to take such a risk.

Believing you have the full story can inspire overconfidence and overstepping. Challenge your understanding by asking yourself, "What do I *not* know in this situation?" Consider other possible interpretations of the facts before you. Most importantly, continue your whole-self observation and allow new information to reshape your understanding when appropriate.

Yeah, but...

"I don't care what other people are doing, thinking or feeling at work. I want to keep to myself, do my work, and not get involved in the drama around me."

I hear you. Dealing with people, in general, is exhausting. I'd rather not do it much of the time! But at work, it's part of the job. As much as we'd like to, we simply can't ignore people. They are an important part of the environment, whether they're clients, coworkers, superiors, or subordinates.

Regardless of your role, your work relies on others—at least to *some* extent. They affect your work in one way or another. If you tune them out, you're going to miss a lot of useful information. You also risk looking self-absorbed and out of sync, which isn't helpful either.

The workplace, by its very nature, is a group environment. Even people who work alone physically still have to interact with other people. It's important to recognize what's going on for them and consider how it might be relevant to you.

That doesn't mean you need to get sucked into so-called drama. The interpersonal ups and downs that inevitably happen within groups are usually not relevant. You shouldn't allow that kind of thing to absorb valuable attention.

However, you also have to be emotionally intelligent enough to understand when interpersonal issues *are* relevant and address them effectively so they don't hinder your ability to do the job.

Having Situational Awareness is not the same thing as being a gossip or a drama queen. It's about appreciating all facets of the environment, including the oh-so-exhausting social aspects.

IN SUMMARY

I remember several years ago speaking to a friend of mine who was, at the time, a liberal arts major in college. While discussing our career aspirations, she said to me, "I just don't want to be some corporate drone."

The image of the zombie-like corporate drone has been a persistent one, especially in modern American culture. It is the embodiment of level 1 awareness: tuned out, robotic, and disengaged.

The response I gave my friend those many years ago is similar to the advice I give now. I told her that I didn't think being a drone was a requirement. Indeed, I've learned it's actually a serious impediment to success.

As humans, we are cognitive creatures. We've been endowed with so many gifts—our brains, our five senses, and our mysterious inner wisdom. When we develop the skill of Situational Awareness, we're choosing to use these gifts purposefully. We already have all the tools required.

From here, we press forward on our proactive journey. But where, exactly, are we going? Why, to the future, of course!

REFLECTION EXERCISES

1. Reflect on an average workday. What percentage of the time do you spend in each level of awareness? (Note: At this point, it's

normal to spend some time in each.) From the outside, what do you think each level looks like to others? How do you think your level of awareness impacts your experiences?

2. Try to identify the kinds of things (situations, people, tasks, and so on) that trigger you to tune out or go into high alert. With this knowledge, take extra care to approach these things mindfully going forward.

CHAPTER 7

FUTURE FOCUS

You have brains in your head. You have feet in your shoes. You can steer yourself in any direction you choose. You're on your own, and you know what to do. And you are the one who'll decide where to go.

Dr. Seuss, American writer and illustrator (1904–1991)

THE THIRD ESSENTIAL component of The Proactive Skillset is Future Focus. This is defined as *the ability to create a clear vision of the future by defining desired results and identifying action items.*

Before we discuss this next crucial step in the proactive journey, let's regroup. So far, you've created your mental map by developing Big Picture Understanding. Then, you identified your place on the map by developing Situational Awareness. Now, you'll begin building on these foundational components to navigate your path forward. But before we get too far, you first must figure out where you want to go.

Let's look at the definition of Future Focus in detail.

The purpose of this skill is to *create a clear vision of the future*. After all, if you're not sure what kind of future you're working toward, you can't do anything meaningful in the present to make it happen. Proactive people set their sights on the destination and, as needed, adjust their sails in the wind to get there. Reactive people, on the other hand, are happy to let the wind carry them where it may. They allow outside influences to dictate the destination.

The rest of the definition explains two essential steps that help create future vision. The first is *defining desired results*. This means understanding the outcomes you want to create for yourself and others.

The second is *identifying action items*. Action items are things you need to do to achieve your desired results. This is a critical part of Future Focus because these things will require your commitment of time, energy, and attention in the future—all of which are in limited supply. You can't make smart decisions about how to use your precious resources if you don't have an accurate and complete view of the actions you'll need to take to achieve your desired results in the future.

Collectively, for our purposes, we'll call these things "goals." Think of it like this:

Desired Results + Action Items = Goals

Goals require both pieces of the equation. Without a course of action, your desired results are worthless. Likewise, engaging in action items without defining desired results is very likely to be ineffective and problematic.

Goals represent where you're going. Future Focus is the skill of creating your goals and keeping a watchful eye on them.

PUSH GOALS VERSUS PULL GOALS

In the workplace, goals come from a variety of sources. Some are simply the built-in demands and obligations of your role. Other people may assign goals to you, and still other goals may be self-assigned.

Often you start with one part of the equation or the other—you either know the desired results you're trying to achieve or you know the action items on your plate. In either case, it's your job to figure out the missing part of the equation.

I call these *push goals* and *pull goals*. If you think about trying to move an object, you can push or pull it. Either one will get the job done. But the mechanism for how it happens is slightly different. The same is true for these types of goals.

A *push goal* is one where the desired results are defined first, but you have to identify the action items to get there. For example, you're tasked with reducing processing time for invoices by 20 percent over the next quarter. You have all the freedom in the world to determine how that happens. However, you don't have a full view of the goal until you've identified the action items associated with it.

A *pull goal* is the opposite—it's one where you've identified the action item but the desired result is unclear. This is particularly common when your role involves a lot of task work or assignments from others.

For example, imagine your boss asks you to take his place at a meeting this afternoon. In typical "boss" fashion, few other details are offered. You've captured the action item, but without knowing the desired result, you only have half the relevant information.

Reactive Rita would simply show up to the meeting as instructed and hope for the best. However, both you and Proactive Patty, with your finely tuned Future Focus skills, know there's another step required. You need to define desired results.

Sometimes you can rely on your existing knowledge and experience, along with the other skills in your proactive toolkit to figure it out. Other times, you might need to have a quick conversation to gain clarity.

In this case of filling in for your boss at the meeting, you might define a list of desired results such as:

- to represent your boss well by showing up on time and being pre-pared to share the status of a few high-profile projects
- to capture all key discussion items to report back to your boss the next day
- to make a positive impression on the other attending executives, including one from another department, which might have some exciting career growth opportunities for you in the future

Just by defining these three outcomes, you'll be better positioned to effectively prepare for the meeting and stay appropriately focused during the meeting. Failing to take this step can lead to missed opportunities, wasted time, and ineffective actions.

Push goals are certainly ideal. Whenever possible, it's best to start with a clearly defined desired result and build action items to get there. But that's just not always possible in the workplace. We're constantly bombarded by a whirlwind of action items inspiring us to shoot first, aim later, and that's exactly how Reactive Rita operates. But with the skill of Future Focus, you learn to pause—even in the middle of the whirlwind—and figure out where you're going.

PARAMETERS OF SUCCESS

I remember a popular radio commercial I frequently heard on my morning commute several years ago. As it started, a booming voice proclaimed, "This commercial is only for people who want to *succeed* in life."

I thought it was pretty clever since, presumably, most people would opt in. As far as I know, failure is seldom a life goal.

However, when we're trying to create a clear vision for the future, "success" is not an adequate description. You must define exactly what *success* means. Otherwise, the destination is too vague. You'll have no way of knowing if or when you actually get there.

Success in any given situation can mean something different. Your version might be very different from mine. Defining your specific success parameters will help you create a more concrete vision for the future and, ultimately, give you the ability to be proactive.

The SMART acronym is a popular tool for goal setting and one most professionals are already comfortable working with. Originally developed in 1981 by a management consultant named George T. Doran, this model proposes that goals should possess the following characteristics:

- **Specific**—The goal states the results you want to achieve or the action you want to accomplish in the most precise terms possible.
- **Measurable**—The goal includes quantifiable measurements that will help you track progress and let you know when it is complete.
- **Achievable**—The goal is reasonable and can be attained *with effort*.
- **Relevant**—The goal matters and is a worthwhile use of resources.
- **Time-Bound**—The goal includes time factors and targets for timely completion.

This simple framework can give substance to *any* endeavor or potential pursuit. It can and should be used when reflecting upon both desired results and action items.

Proactive Patty is attending a multiday industry conference as a representative of her organization. Using the SMART methodology, she defines the following desired result:

- to generate at least three promising leads for potential new business by the end of the conference

To support this outcome, she identifies her first action item as the following:

- to introduce herself and her organization to at least ten new people on the first day of the conference

From here, Patty can continue identifying action items to support her desired result. With these goals in mind, she'll have appropriate Future Focus for the purposes of the conference.

In the workplace, some success parameters are clearly assigned to you—deadlines, budgets, and so on. Others are not so clear, and you'll have to do a little digging to uncover them. Yet others may be of your own creation, based on your personal or professional ambitions, to design a more comprehensive view of your desired future.

VIEWING THE FULL HORIZON

Examining the wide-open territory of "the future" without any organization or structure can be an overwhelming task. While the goal of Future Focus is to develop the most complete view possible, that doesn't mean you have to look at it all at once. Instead, it helps to look at the future, as well as your goals, in chunks.

Imagine looking out a window at your home and gazing into the distance. With perfect vision, your eyes are able to take in the entire landscape, near and far and the space in between, from a wide perspective. However, you're also able to shift your focus on command. You can look at the beautiful garden in your own front yard. You can look at your neighbor's garden—not nearly as nice as yours. You can watch the kids playing down the street or even shift your eyes and enjoy the gently rolling hills backlit by the setting sun behind them.

This kind of "full horizon" perspective is the goal of Future Focus. To get there, it helps to first think of the future and your goals along separate horizons that ultimately connect to create a complete view.

1. THE VISIONARY HORIZON

The first horizon is that of the distant future—a year or more from now. As its name indicates, defining results and identifying action items this far into the future requires vision and sometimes even a touch of imagination. Your personal and professional goals at this horizon collectively act as your north star. You should always be moving (sometimes gently, sometimes aggressively) toward achieving these things.

2. THE STRATEGIC HORIZON

The second horizon covers the middle territory, and we typically look at it in chunks of time that are anywhere from one to three months out. We call this horizon "strategic" because the goals here are approaching but aren't directly upon us. We have time to plan, align our decisions, and take appropriate proactive action.

3. THE TACTICAL HORIZON

The third horizon deals with that of the near future—the results we want to create and actions we need to take in the next day, week, or even few minutes. We call this the "tactical" horizon because this is where we are, or soon will be, making decisions and taking action directly in support of our immediate goals.

The three horizons are used to organize how you think about the future and what you want to create at each step. Understanding them helps you think incrementally about your goals in all directions. From the visionary horizon, you're able to look backward and align shorter-term strategic and tactical goals to help you get there. From the tactical horizon, you're able to look forward and ensure you're aiming in the right direction for achieving your longer-term goals.

Obviously, the visionary horizon might be a little hazy at times. The closer things get to the tactical horizon, the clearer they become, and that's perfectly fine. You don't need all the details when you're gazing that far out into the distance. Just the general outline is enough.

It isn't effective to focus solely on one horizon while ignoring the others. Though the tactical horizon is the closest and often becomes quite cluttered in the workplace, the other horizons persistently edge closer with each passing moment. If we don't stay mindful, they sneak up on us. Without regular attention, the further-out goals end up neglected, and when they inevitably appear on the tactical horizon, we have no choice but to reactively jump into action. Our time for proactivity by then has passed.

The full horizon framework provides a useful reminder of the multilayered nature of goals in the workplace. The process of monitoring all horizons helps ensure we're making intelligent decisions and taking the right action to support success in both the short- and long-term future.

DEVELOPING FUTURE FOCUS

At this point, we've established that Future Focus requires setting and monitoring goals with specific success parameters across the full horizon.

So how do we do that?

First, you might need to make a small but important mental adjustment. Many professionals think of goal setting as an event, something they do around the start of a new year or in preparation for a performance review. Few actually see it as an ongoing process. Those who have a strong sense of Future Focus are *always* goal setting. It's not an activity reserved for certain times or special situations. It's a daily—even moment-to-moment—practice.

Much like proactivity itself, developing this skill is a process that involves both physical and mental engagement. Over time, it becomes second nature. But in the beginning, it requires concentrated effort. The following strategies have proven helpful.

CAPTURE AND CLARIFY

In order to develop Future Focus, you must learn to constantly *capture* and *clarify* goals—both desired results and action items.

Capture means to catch them and not let them slip away. In the workplace, goals are thrown at us all day long. It's easy to miss, or simply forget, something important.

For example, during a hallway chat, your boss briefly mentions a project he'd like you to oversee next month. At this point, it's a pull goal since you have a high-level action item but haven't yet defined any desired results, and it lives on the strategic horizon for now. However, it's still something you need to capture, as it will definitely impact your future. On the tactical horizon, you might also capture an action item to follow up with your boss in the next few days to get the details.

It's beyond the scope of this book to offer guidance regarding what system to use for capturing your desired results and action items, except to say that you *do* need a system. It's your choice whether to use good, old-fashioned pen and paper, some kind of fancy software, or a hybrid of the two (as I prefer).

Clarify means to make your goals clear and unambiguous. Asking questions of yourself and others is the best way to ensure your goals have all the SMART elements.

- **Specific**—What do I need to accomplish? What do I want to achieve?
- **Measurable**—How will I track progress and know this goal is complete (i.e., how much, how many, and so on)?
- **Achievable**—Is this goal achievable with effort? If not, consider revision.

THE PROACTIVE PROFESSIONAL

- **Relevant**—Does this goal matter? If not, consider revision.
- **Time-Bound**—What time factors do I need to consider? What is my target for completion?

Proactive people ask these questions repeatedly—so often, in fact, that it just becomes a natural part of the way they think. They never approach anything in the workplace, be it a complicated project or a simple task, without at least considering the SMART components.

Let's expand on our earlier example for just a minute.

Proactive Patty has just bumped into her boss in the hallway and discovered he'd like her to oversee a project next month. She captures this as a high-level pull goal and sets an additional goal to meet with him at a later date. In essence, her desired results for the meeting are to capture and clarify desired results for the project.

Initiating this meeting is already a proactive goal, but Patty goes a step further and applies the SMART methodology to it.

In terms of *specifics*, she wants a meeting to learn some details about the project she's overseeing.

For *measurables*, Patty draws up a list of questions she needs answered about the project. She knows that, if all her questions are answered, she can call this particular goal complete.

She then considers the *time factors*. Her boss mentioned the project starts next month. Patty wants enough time to prepare for the project and also knows her boss is headed out of town in two weeks. So she creates an "artificial" deadline for herself to

87

make sure the meeting happens by no later than Wednesday of next week.

Finally, Patty quickly checks for *achievability* and *relevance* and determines that, yes, her goal is sound.

If Reactive Rita had been in the same position, we all know what would have happened. The conversation in the hallway wouldn't have registered as anything of note, and she wouldn't have proactively set a meeting with her boss. In fact, she probably wouldn't have realized a meeting was even necessary until right when the boss was out of town and the project set to begin! Chances are pretty good that, if and when the meeting finally took place, she wouldn't have created that clear list of questions to ask either.

The SMART methodology might feel like overkill for some smaller tasks, but they are goals like any other. In order to reach success, you need to clarify the destination.

Lastly, it's worthwhile mentioning that, while the SMART methodology steers us in the right direction, it also stops us from accidentally heading in the wrong direction.

Using its framework, the S, M, and T are the elements that add meat to the bones of your goals. However, the A and R are still very useful, especially with regard to proactivity. If you're facing a goal that doesn't appear achievable (with effort) or relevant, it's a good indication that some new action is required. You might need to renegotiate one or more elements of the S, M, or T, or you might need to reexamine the purpose of the goal altogether, possibly with the help of a manager.

Learning how to capture and clarify your goals is the first essential step to developing Future Focus.

PLAN ACROSS THE HORIZON

Planning is the process of regularly reviewing all of your goals and formulating strategies to achieve them.

According to Brian Tracy, one of the world's most popular personal development experts, "Every minute you spend planning saves ten minutes in execution." The act of planning is, by its very nature, proactive.

Of course, life seldom goes perfectly according to plan. But even that doesn't negate the power of the process.

Through planning, you're able to do a number of different things, including the following:

- consider desired results and establish action items to achieve them
- review action items and consider other actions they may produce
- break down large goals into smaller ones
- recognize the necessary sequencing of action items by identifying dependencies (actions that rely on one another)
- consider capacity and ensure your goals remain achievable

In short, the planning process gives you time to think about what you need to do and achieve from a bird's eye view. Regular planning helps keep goals top of mind, focuses attention appropriately, and reduces stress.

The planning process need not be an overly complicated or time-consuming one—provided that it takes place *consistently*. The goal is to look at the full horizon but, as mentioned earlier, not necessarily all at once in extreme detail.

Once again, it's beyond the scope of this book to provide in-depth guidance for planning. There are plenty of time management books and other resources available that do this far better than I ever could. However, the strategies I offer will ensure your process accomplishes the fundamental things required for building the skill of Future Focus and positioning yourself for being proactive at work.

First, and most importantly, the process of planning must become a cherished and protected ritual in your professional life. Planning time should be uninterrupted—a short period during which you can truly focus on the task at hand. Many people find it helpful to schedule recurring appointments on the calendar specifically for this purpose.

To achieve a full horizon perspective, planning should be done at regular intervals including (at a minimum) the following:

- annually
- quarterly
- monthly
- weekly
- daily

A solid planning process should include three steps: review, prioritize, schedule.

REVIEW

The review component involves a quick appraisal of both the past and the future.

The first part of the process might seem counterintuitive for building Future Focus. But you can't be certain about where you want to go if you aren't also clear on where you've already been.

The point of reviewing the past is twofold. First, you need to identify the goals you've already achieved and no longer need to devote resources to. But you're also looking for lessons. You're connecting the dots of the past to determine what will and won't work for achieving goals in the future.

Perhaps you discovered in the past that a goal was not met because unexpected delays caused you to miss the deadline. Next time you work on a similar goal, you'll know to build a little buffer room into the schedule. (Note: this is *always* a good idea!) Or maybe you discovered that working with a certain person on your team posed a specific set of challenges in achieving a past goal, and you take note that next time you'll approach the process of collaboration with this person differently. In the next chapter, we discuss the specific thought processes involved.

Reviewing the future involves gathering all of the various goals that still need your attention and taking note of any commitments already on the calendar, such as specific meetings, deadlines, appointments, events, travel, and so on.

The planning interval should dictate how far into the horizon this future review takes you. For example, on a daily basis, you're monitoring the tactical horizon—the day in front of you, the next few days, and perhaps up to a week. Once a week, you're looking at the next couple of weeks. On a monthly and quarterly basis, you're reviewing the strategic horizon, and on an annual or biannual basis, you're assessing the visionary horizon.

While these aren't hard-and-fast rules, such a structure helps ensure all horizons get regular attention.

At any stage, the future review process should ultimately lead back to the tactical horizon. The purpose is always to ask, *"What can I do in the near-term to increase my chances of success in the long-term?"*

This simple question represents one of the most powerful steps you can take toward becoming proactive. It encourages you to look ahead and then work your way backward.

PRIORITIZE

Once you have a full horizon perspective of your goals, the next part of the planning process is to prioritize them. *Prioritization* means to determine the order for execution. This is usually based on a combination of factors, including *importance* (a consideration of value) and *urgency* (a consideration of time).

In his bestselling book, *The 7 Habits of Highly Effective People*, author Steven Covey uses the Time Management Matrix in figure 4 to map these two crucial elements for prioritizing.

FIGURE 4. TIME MANAGEMENT MATRIX

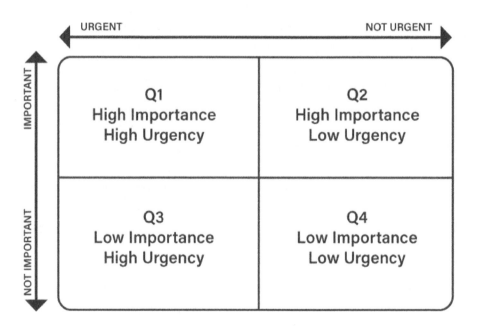

Quadrant one (Q1) represents goals that have both *high importance* and *high urgency*. These are critical items that, left unattended, would result in seriously negative consequences. When we're stuck in reactivity, this is where our focus is 100 percent of the time. We're running from fire to fire, managing by crisis, dealing with the next highly urgent, highly important item to show up on our desk.

Quadrant two (Q2) is for goals that are *important but not urgent*—this is where planning actually lives, along with personal development and other goals that are indeed important for future success but lack immediacy. By doing important things when they're not urgent, we're being proactive about the future. We can often prevent goals from transitioning into Q1 territory by focusing on them early when they're still in Q2. Neglecting Q2 activities eventually yields more Q1 activities, creating the trappings of a vicious reactivity cycle.

Whenever possible, proactive people prioritize Q2 activities. Of course, that doesn't mean you can ignore Q1 activities—far from it, in fact. You're always going to have to manage these things. But you must *also* consciously turn your attention to Q2. This is what reactive people fail to do.

Quadrant three (Q3) and quadrant four (Q4) represent low importance activities and should therefore be deprioritized, minimized, and avoided whenever possible.

SCHEDULE

The final step in the planning process is to schedule your action items by assigning a specific date and time in the future in which you will complete them.

Scheduling is not an exact science. Just because an action item is scheduled doesn't mean it can't be rescheduled. However, the process of scheduling, in and of itself, is a valuable tool for proactivity because it forces you to do a number of different things.

First, scheduling means making a commitment. Activities that are scheduled are more likely to be accomplished and less likely to be forgotten or procrastinated. A block of time is designated for a specific action item, which helps prevent distraction.

Scheduling also requires that you consider how long each action item will take and what can realistically be done in any given period of time. This kind of assessment helps you manage your resources, such as time and energy, more effectively.

When estimating time for any action item, it's useful to include a *safety margin*—additional time to deal with the unexpected. Generally speaking, a 50 percent safety margin is a good starting point. For example, if you're scheduling time to complete a task that will take two hours if all goes smoothly, block three hours to account for Murphy's Law.[3] You may choose to adjust this (increasing or decreasing the safety margin) based on your own best judgment.

Finally, effective scheduling requires a clear understanding of how your goals interact with one another and how action items must be sequenced.

For example, imagine you need to write a proposal recommending a new software solution for your group. Before that can be done, however, you need to first investigate at least three viable options. Obviously, your schedule should reflect all of the required action items in the correct order. You wouldn't schedule time to write the proposal before first scheduling time to research your options.

It's also important to schedule "free time" to ensure you're still able to meet unforeseen demands and accommodate last-minute requests. These things are an inescapable part of the nature of the workplace. The amount of time required for this designation will vary depending on your role.

---

3 Anything that *can* go wrong *will*.

With the help of scheduling, you can create a detailed view of your *desired* future—exactly what you need to do and when—to achieve your goals. Reality won't always align perfectly, and that's OK. You must remain adaptable and flex when needed. The goal is simply to start from a place of clarity.

Yeah, but...

"The previous skill (Situational Awareness) is all about focusing on the present, but now we're told to focus on the future. Which is it?"

It's both! I realize that might sound like a contradiction, but it's not. The human brain is a wonderfully complicated thing. I'm often amazed at what it can do, and this is a perfect example.

The skill of proactivity is multifaceted and requires the ability to look at the world from many different angles at once. The good news is that your brain is more than capable of doing this. I'm not a neuroscientist, so I can't explain the mechanism by which it works (nor would you, dear reader, care for that level of detail, I'm quite certain).

I can, however, attest to the fact that as humans, we have the ability to consciously shift our attention from the past to the present to the future in mere fractions of a second. It's like a cool form of mental time travel.

The brain also has the ability to manage complex webs of information all at once. We can pay attention to where we are without losing sight of where we're going and vice versa. It's not an either/or proposition. And in fact, this incredibly elaborate cognitive capability is part of what makes proactivity possible in the first place.

IN SUMMARY

Several years ago, I became fascinated with the game of pool. To be clear, I was an exceptionally bad player and still am. My fascination was born out of the realization that every good pool player I encountered seemed to be engaged in an entirely different game from the one I was playing.

They were strategic, where I was spontaneous. No matter where the cue ball started, these expert players were able to line things up perfectly so that a chain of events would take place, ultimately sinking the ball they originally intended to sink. They were precise and methodical, and nothing ever seemed to surprise them. For me, any random ball landing in any random pocket triggered a bouncy squeal of disbelief.

Whenever I think of Future Focus, I think of people who are really good at pool. It's a very similar skill. Future Focus is all about keeping your eye on the ball and the pocket you're aiming for and mapping out the chain of events that needs to take place to bring them together. When we hone this skill, we're able to set ourselves up for success no matter what. It's not random chance; it's strategy.

Of course, the pool analogy also brings us to our next skill, Strategic Foresight, because that's what makes the expert pool player *really* effective. It's not enough to set your goal and map out the chain of events that needs to take place; you also need to understand how that chain works. In pool, it's simple geometry. If you hit a ball at a certain angle, you can expect it to move in a predictable way. When playing the game, you must anticipate these movements and account for them in your setup.

The same is true in the proactive journey. As we line ourselves up to reach our destination with Future Focus, we must use the next skill, Strategic

Foresight, to anticipate predictable outcomes and prepare for potential obstacles. This knowledge is what helps ensure we're properly set up for success.

Now that you understand Future Focus, let's move on to this next exciting step in the journey.

⌣⌐

REFLECTION EXERCISES

1. Review your current systems for managing goals. Consider all aspects—how do you capture, clarify, plan, review, prioritize, and schedule? Are your systems adequate? What improvements can you make to ensure your Future Focus remains clear?

2. Review your current goals and verify they are SMART. Do you have any push goals or pull goals on the horizon? Practice using what you've learned! Turn them into complete goals by defining desired results, identifying action items, and setting success parameters.

CHAPTER 8

STRATEGIC FORESIGHT

We cannot solve problems by using the same kind of thinking we used when we created them.

ALBERT EINSTEIN, GERMAN THEORETICAL PHYSICIST (1879–1955)

THE FOURTH ESSENTIAL component of The Proactive Skillset is Strategic Foresight. This is defined as *the ability to use logic and imagination to anticipate opportunities, obstacles, and outcomes.*

Once again, let's reestablish where we are in the proactive journey. At this point, you've built your map (Big Picture Understanding) and found your place on it (Situational Awareness). You've set your sights on the destination (Future Focus), and you're ready to forge ahead!

But the path before you is dark. Your job now is to shine a light on it and see what you can see. You must look for signs, indications to turn this way or that, warnings of danger or good things ahead. You must determine if this path is familiar or one you've never seen before. With this information, you'll be able to prepare for your journey and plan your movements to ensure safe and efficient passage to your destination.

I often tell my training participants this is where the magic happens. Strategic Foresight is what makes The Proactive Skillset so powerful. It's also the skill most lacking in the average professional.

Colin Powell, former Secretary of State and retired four-star army general, once advised leaders to look for people who have "a capacity to see around corners." This is perhaps the best description I've seen for the skill of Strategic Foresight. But don't let it scare you off! We're not talking about supernatural powers here. What lies around any given "corner" is always a mystery. But Strategic Foresight helps us manage the uncertainty of the future by thinking about what *could* be and what's *likely* to be and planning appropriately.

Let's start our exploration of this rare skill by discussing what it actually means.

The definition provided earlier has a few key components. First, it specifies the use of both *logic* and *imagination*. Albert Einstein said, "Logic will take you from A to B. Imagination will take you everywhere." Put another way, logic is linear and limited to what we know and understand, while imagination is wild and limitless.

When it comes to being proactive, I do not believe that logic is inherently better than imagination or vice versa, nor are they mutually exclusive. In fact, it is the combination that creates true magic. We can imagine entire new worlds, but without logic, we create entertaining fantasies at best—deceptive, frustrating, and senseless illusions at worst. In the 1960s, imagination inspired our trip to the moon, but logic made it possible and a viable goal worth working toward. Together, logic and imagination form the secret sauce of Strategic Foresight.

With this skill, we use that secret sauce for a very specific purpose—*to anticipate opportunities, obstacles, and outcomes.*

Opportunities represent a gap between the real and imagined, *obstacles* the potential problems that stand in the way, and *outcomes* the results. *Anticipating* these things means we're evaluating what's possible and what's probable and making intelligent calculations about what to expect in the future.

In short, this is the skill of looking ahead and asking, "What next?" With such insight, we're able to make better choices regarding our path forward (choices that are more likely to lead to success) and pre-emptively manage, minimize, or avoid trouble along the way. This is the very essence of proactivity!

In my experience, the idea of Strategic Foresight can spark some resistance in people. At first, it might sound like we're attempting to do the impossible—to truly predict the future. The cynic might say it sounds more like "guessing." In fact, Strategic Foresight is a skill, not some mystical power or a game of darts. *It's a thoughtful and informed estimation.*

It's also worth noting that certain opportunities, obstacles, and outcomes are indeed so common as to be essentially predictable to any casual observer. It requires little effort, for example, to estimate that travel itineraries will frequently encounter delays, especially in the winter months when weather can be especially unpredictable. It requires little effort to anticipate that attempting to squeeze fifty hours of work into a forty-hour workweek will lead to stress, exhaustion, and potential failure. These things are not difficult to see, and indeed predict, if you take a moment to employ a little logic and imagination.

THE POSITIVE SIDE OF PATTERNS

In chapter 6, we discussed the paradox of patterns and why it's important to avoid the negative traps patterns can create by developing Situational Awareness.

However, patterns are (paradoxically!) helpful tools for developing the skill of Strategic Foresight. Thoughtfully used, they can provide advanced notice of what's to come.

A *pattern* in the workplace is a routine or a sequence of events based on cause and effect. To use them intelligently, we must utilize our deductive and inductive reasoning skills.

Deductive reasoning starts with a general assumption and applies it to a specific event. Deductive reasoning says, "I've experienced this pattern in the past; therefore, I'm likely to experience it in this similar situation I'm facing now."

For example, in the past, customers who purchased Product A have had problems understanding the instructions for setup. *(This is the pattern.)* Therefore, when you're working with a customer who has just purchased Product A, you can guess that he will probably have problems understanding the instructions as well. With deductive reasoning, you can take proactive action by clarifying instructions ahead of time or working to resolve the bigger underlying issue of the confusing instructions.

As long as the general assumption is accurate, deductive reasoning works quite well.

Inductive reasoning is the opposite. It starts with a specific event and creates a general assumption for the future. Inductive reasoning says, "I've just experienced this cause and effect; therefore, I'm likely to experience the same pattern in situations like this in the future."

For example, you've just experienced conflict with a coworker while working on a project together. In retrospect, you see that the conflict happened because your individual roles in the project were not defined. Therefore, to avoid conflict with a colleague when working on a project in the future, you know to define roles early on in the process.

Because inductive reasoning creates new patterns, it is more likely to be problematic. You may need to adjust your patterns as you go. For example, if you define roles early on in project work with a colleague and still encounter conflict, you need to adjust. Perhaps this time the conflict was due to overly aggressive deadlines. Therefore, your new pattern becomes: to avoid conflict with a colleague while working on a project, define roles early on *and* keep deadlines reasonable.

As humans, we are pattern-seeking creatures. Our brains naturally fill in the blanks and connect the dots with logic. Proactive people use this capability intelligently to assess the situation and better understand the likely consequences of their actions.

Still, patterns are not perfectly consistent, and they shouldn't be treated as exact science. They merely provide a baseline for expectations. We must continue to use our Situational Awareness to watch for anomalies—telltale signs that a pattern might *not* hold true in any given circumstance.

THE POWER OF IMAGINATION

Some situations don't fit an existing pattern, nor are they indicative of future patterns. They are simply unique.

But that doesn't mean they're entirely unpredictable. The world itself tends to behave rationally—even in unusual circumstances. The basic laws of cause and effect still apply.

With the help of your Big Picture Understanding and your broader professional experience and wisdom, you can use logic to speculate about the future. In essence, you can *imagine* where various paths lead, even when traveling in completely foreign territory.

This isn't a new idea. The military has used scenario-based games for hundreds of years to hone strategies and practice various models of warfare. It's a helpful training tool because it forces participants to think about what they would do *if* certain things happened. As they "play," they develop a greater understanding of cause and effect, which builds a strong foundation for Strategic Foresight in the real world.

This is also something you've probably done naturally throughout your life. You've likely played certain scenarios out in your head:

If I don't finish these materials by noon, I'll miss the cutoff for the FedEx pickup.

If I miss the cutoff, I'll have to go downtown to the FedEx drop box.

My last meeting ends at 4:30, so if I have to go downtown, I'll get stuck right in the middle of rush hour traffic.

If I get stuck in rush hour traffic, I could miss the cutoff for the drop box too.

If I miss FedEx entirely today, I'll have to ship the materials tomorrow.

If I can't ship the materials until tomorrow, we'll have to reschedule the presentation.

And so on...

When you imagine how certain events might unfold, you're using Strategic Foresight. When you backtrack and use that information to make smarter decisions and take more effective action today, you're being proactive.

It's Strategic Foresight that gives you the power to pre-empt problems, create contingency plans, and find alternative routes that lead to your desired destination. Using it helps you create a more intentional future, setting into motion the chain of events you *want* versus merely reacting to the chain of events that occurs.

For example, in the previous scenario, you could proactively (1) determine what would stop you from finishing the materials by noon and prevent those problems, (2) cancel your last meeting of the day so you can get downtown earlier if needed, or (3) ask someone else in the office to take your package downtown earlier in the day. And that's only a small fraction of the options available.

Note: We'll talk more about the decision-making and action-taking part of the process in the next chapter. Strategic Foresight is the thought process that takes place first.

Strategic Foresight is most useful when it's used to generate *realistic* ideas of what's to come. Downward-spiral thinking isn't helpful.

Notice in the previous example that we don't jump from missing the FedEx pickup to being fired and living on the streets eating dog food. In most workplaces, that's not a logical leap. There are likely many more steps in a chain of events that leads from one to the other and many opportunities along the way to prevent such a disastrous outcome.

The purpose of these thought experiments is not to cause needless worry, but rather, to simply imagine possible opportunities, obstacles, and outcomes in order to better prepare for the future. Leaping to illogical catastrophic conclusions only hinders your ability to think clearly and act intelligently.

Remember too that any imagined scenario is merely speculation. It's *one* way the future *may* unfold. It's not a guarantee. The action you take in the present is what creates the future—not the other way around. Your goal is to align your present-day action with the future you desire. To do so, you must take the variables into account so you can choose the most probable path for success.

THE DOMINO EFFECT
At its core, Strategic Foresight is about understanding consequences and recognizing that every situation begets a web of possible opportunities, obstacles, and outcomes.

In any given moment, we face choices—each a potential path leading to a different destination. Like an elaborate domino maze, every choice we make sets off a chain reaction, creating new situations and new webs of possibilities.

Nothing happens in a vacuum, especially in the workplace. Your work impacts the work of others and the results of the organization as a whole. Your choices have a far-reaching effect. They ripple outward, shaping your future and the futures of others.

Reactive people are constantly knocking down the dominoes. They watch the pieces fall one by one and wonder what happened to create such a mess. Proactive people, conversely, understand the game and the immense responsibility of it. They think carefully before setting off that chain reaction.

Surprises can still happen, of course. Goodness knows a domino you thought would fall left can unexpectedly fall right. Surprises can't be completely eliminated even with perfect Strategic Foresight. *How* the dominoes will fall is never 100 percent predictable, but the fact that they *will* fall is.

DEVELOPING STRATEGIC FORESIGHT
The skill of Strategic Foresight is really a by-product of the first three skills. If you've already worked to develop Big Picture Understanding, Situational Awareness, and Future Focus, this will be a natural next step in your development.

As you've learned, Strategic Foresight relies on deductive and inductive reasoning, as well as logic and imagination. For some, these abilities are simply innate. However, there are still steps you can take to cultivate the skill and tools to facilitate a greater level of reliability in the process.

ESTABLISH PROCEDURES
Establishing procedures means giving structure to the things you do regularly, sometimes (though not always) by writing the steps down.

Doing this helps develop Strategic Foresight because procedures clearly define the chain of events required to get you to your desired destination with a given task. They offer a peek into the future and provide more ability to manage variables.

Procedures are, by nature, designed to create predictable outcomes and circumvent potential obstacles. They define the way things should be done if all goes according to plan and may also include contingency plans for what to do if and when things veer off course.

One quick note: Don't get hung up on the word itself. A *procedure* need not be formal; it doesn't need to use any specific format or look a certain way, and it doesn't need to be approved by anyone else. While writing them down is often useful for memory's sake, especially when something is repeated infrequently, there may be times when a procedure is simply a mental note regarding how things should be done. Whatever works for you is good enough, as long as you understand it and can rely on it when needed. If you prefer, replace the word *procedure* with something else like *system, routine, process,* or *guideline.*

Procedures prevent you from having to recreate the wheel every time you engage in a task or recreate the path every time you aim for a familiar destination. If something is likely to be done more than once, establish a procedure for it just in case. You never know when it will appear again.

Checklists, templates, and flow charts can all be used to outline the steps involved in a procedure. When establishing and leveraging procedures in the workplace, consider these questions:

- Is this situation similar to others like it that I've already experienced? If so, rely on established procedure.
- Is this situation indicative of future situations? If so, create a new procedure.

One key point about procedures should not be overlooked: they are always subject to change. A perfect procedure will help you reach predictable outcomes every time. But of course, perfection is an unrealistic aim. If a procedure is getting the wrong results or creating obstacles rather than circumventing them, it needs to be revised. Don't blindly rely on procedures that aren't working. Change them.

Given the wide variety of situations you probably face in the workplace, it is likely impossible to proceduralize every possibility. And really, that's not the goal. Rather, the idea is simply to think about the steps involved in any given process *before* jumping in and to use what you already know to increase the likelihood of producing positive outcomes now and in the future.

To illustrate these ideas, allow me to offer two examples from my personal experience.

EXAMPLE 1

While attending college, I briefly waited tables at a restaurant that was located right next door to a busy movie theater. Within my first few weeks on the job, I noticed a common occurrence among several groups of diners. As the end of the meal approached, they began to look worried and frazzled. I'd ask them if they had saved room for dessert, and they'd hastily explain they were trying to catch a movie and needed to wrap things up *now*.

Obviously, as a server, I was living on tips. Having a stressed out customer rush for the door wasn't exactly how I wanted the meal to end. It didn't take long to realize that I needed to change my approach. I learned the pattern and established a new procedure.

"Hi! My name is Chrissy, and I'll be your server tonight. May I ask if you're planning to catch a movie after your meal?"

This is how I started approaching every table during the prime movie-going hours. If they were indeed on a schedule, my response was almost always the same: "Great! I'll do my best to make sure you can relax and enjoy your meal and still catch the previews."

Now, if you've ever waited tables in a restaurant, you know that there are a great many things outside of your control. I couldn't guarantee that the timing would work perfectly—especially since a surprising number of diners really underestimated how long it would take to get a table.

However, I found that simply by asking the question, I was able to offer my diners a sense of peace. I was on their side, and I had all the necessary information. At least I knew what I was up against! I could do everything in my power to manage the time constraints effectively, and even if they still ended up rushing in the end, they knew I had tried my best.

EXAMPLE 2

A few years later, while working as an executive assistant, I was assigned to oversee a company-wide, multiday, offsite retreat. This was an enormous project, involving a lot of research and decision making. I handled everything from venue selection and travel arrangements to meal planning and setting the agenda.

When it was all over, I had a file full of paperwork and a great accomplishment under my belt. I also had no idea if or when I'd ever be asked to do something like this again (there was no established pattern). However, I decided it was better to be safe than sorry.

After the event wrapped up, I spent a little time organizing my materials and making notes for the future. While it was all still fresh in my mind, I wanted to establish some procedures just in case I ever faced such a daunting task again. I had learned a lot and knew I could minimize my stress in the future by turning those lessons into something tangible—something I could refer back to if or when it was ever needed.

Most people wouldn't have bothered doing this. They would have set the file aside (or worse, trashed it!) and moved on to the next thing immediately.

As luck would have it, after this experience, I was indeed called upon to handle a wide variety of other corporate events. Each time, I not only relied on my procedures but also continued to fine-tune them, updating them with new lessons learned. The small amount of time it took to organize my procedures was far outweighed by their usefulness.

By the time I left that position, I had managed dozens of large-scale, high-profile events and developed exceptionally well-crafted procedural documents, which I happily passed on to my successor.

I didn't know it at the time, but in each situation, I was using Strategic Foresight. I gazed at the path ahead, made reasonable predictions about what was to come, and adapted my behavior to accommodate. It wasn't rocket science, and it required only minimal effort.

ASK, "WHAT IF?"

While Strategic Foresight relies on understanding patterns and using logic, it also requires imagination, which is where this next strategy comes in.

As a kid, my friends and I used to play the "What If" game. The premise was simple: We'd come up with various scenarios for one another ("What if your parents decided to move to Japan?" or "What if everything you touch turned to chocolate?"), and the other player would have to figure out what she'd do. It was a silly way to pass the time, imagining bizarre situations and equally bizarre responses.

Odd as it sounds, you can play a similar game with yourself in the workplace to enhance your Strategic Foresight.

Any question that begins with "What if..." is powerful. It forces you to pause and consider the obstacles and opportunities that may exist in the future. *What if X happens? What if Y is possible?* Searching for the answer requires you to consider cause and effect, as well as the resources at your disposal. *What would I do if X happened? What would I need to do to make Y possible?* The exploration process mentally prepares you for the possibilities ahead.

"What if" questions can help you explore what might go wrong and then work backward to determine how to prevent it. Remember, we're not trying to dwell in the problem; we're using this thought process as a launching pad for problem solving.

Imagine, for example, that you're scheduled to deliver an important presentation to the executive leadership committee in a few days. You've worked on your slides and speech for several weeks and are quite proud.

"What if the projector in the conference room isn't working?" you ask.

With this in mind, you make it a priority to test the projector the day before the meeting to—you hope—resolve any problems early. As a backup, you also print the slides to use as handouts just in case there's an unforeseeable issue and briefly run through how you'd adjust the speech if the projector isn't working at all.

This one simple what if question inspired a series of proactive choices designed to prevent and prepare for potential obstacles. (Note that this would be an especially relevant question if the projector were already known to be temperamental.) Through this process, you would gain peace of mind and increase your odds for a positive outcome, regardless of what happened with the projector. In the end, hopefully, checking the projector and printing the slides would simply become a part of your "important presentation prep" procedure.

Of course, what if questions can also help you to explore potential *positive* future outcomes and help you backtrack to determine how to make them happen.

Imagine approaching a task and asking, "What if there's a better or faster way to do this?"

Such questions inspire innovation. The human brain loves a good puzzle. When you present it with an interesting question, it can't help but attempt to find an answer. Posing this kind of hypothetical possibility signals the brain to start thinking creatively to figure out how it might be done.

Exploring "what if" helps you apply what you already know in new and different ways. It reminds you that, no matter what obstacles arise, your response is always a choice. And while the future remains fluid and outside of your control, these questions remind you of your powerful position of influence. With the help of Strategic Foresight, you can look ahead, consider the consequences of various decisions and actions, and choose intelligently.

Let's reunite with Proactive Patty and Reactive Rita to see this strategy in action.

Both Patty and Rita have a lot going on. They've made a lot of commitments to a lot of different people, and their to-do lists are overflowing. But of course, that doesn't stop the requests from continuing to come in!

One day, their respective bosses invite them to a meeting to discuss a new high-profile project.

"This is a great opportunity," the bosses say. "But I know you're busy and the deadline we're aiming for is aggressive. Is this something you'd like to take on?"

Reactive Rita immediately jumps at the request. She knows there's a lot on her plate right now, but figures the pieces will fall into place as she goes. She wants to be a team player, and, after all, this is a great opportunity.

A few weeks into it, however, Rita is overwhelmed. Her other projects have fallen through the cracks as she struggles to get the new one going. Before long, she clearly sees that the deadline for the new project is unrealistic. By then, she's already failed to deliver on several other commitments as a result of her scattered focus. Others who had relied on her are now struggling to pick up the pieces, and her reputation is taking a major hit. Because of her backlog, the entire department is struggling. Looking back at it, Rita deeply regrets her decision to accept the new project—and so does her boss.

Patty, on the other hand, receives the same request from her boss and runs through a few quick scenarios: *What if I take on this new project with this very ambitious deadline? What will that realistically look like for me and my other priorities?*

These questions help Patty immediately identify a number of potential obstacles and dangerous outcomes. As it is, she's already working several hours of overtime each week. A project like this could add many more, and Patty knows that's not sustainable for long. She'd have to reprioritize some of her existing workload to make the deadline possible. And many other people are relying on her to follow through on her existing promises. If she lets them down, there could be far-reaching consequences, both inside and outside her department, and her credibility could be damaged.

She then asks another question: *What if there is a way to be successful with this project without dropping the ball on my other work?*

This question helps Patty look for opportunities and workarounds. She quickly considers the options and decides it is possible, but she'll need to be strategic to avoid the potential pitfalls.

As a result of this thought process, Patty opens up a conversation with her boss. She tells him she's excited to take on the new project but wants to ensure she's successful. Is there any flexibility on the deadline? Her boss acknowledges that there could be and asks what would be reasonable. Patty suggests a new deadline and assures him she can meet it, provided she can enlist her colleague, Craig, to help on a different project that is expected to take much of her time over the next few weeks. Her boss agrees, and Patty leaves the meeting feeling confident.

Several weeks later, Patty completes the project ahead of schedule. Her proposed deadline gave her more than enough time, and both Patty and her boss are pleasantly surprised that all goes smoothly. With the help of Craig, Patty is able to keep up with her other projects as well. Reflecting on the "great opportunity" her boss promised, Patty is pleased with her decision to make it work.

This example highlights the critical importance of Strategic Foresight and beautifully demonstrates another part of The Proactive Skillset as well,

Intentional Action (discussed in the next chapter). Let's look at some of the things Patty did right.

- Patty anticipated that the deadline would not work and, unlike Rita, chose to renegotiate it from the beginning. She didn't simply accept it, and she didn't wait for it to become a problem. In opening up the conversation right from the very beginning, she found there was indeed flexibility that Rita never explored.
- Patty took into account that there might be unforeseen obstacles. The new deadline she requested strategically provided some wiggle room just in case. When no obstacles appeared, she was able to exceed expectations and finish early.
- Patty recognized that her resources would be stretched thin with this new project, and she didn't want her other priorities to get neglected. Rather than ignore her very reasonable human limitations (as Rita did), Patty requested the help of a colleague.
- Patty's Strategic Foresight helped her determine what kind of commitment she could accept. As Rita discovered, a "great opportunity" can turn into a major disaster when you don't really understand what you're getting into. Patty thought it through carefully and helped establish reasonable expectations before agreeing to the project.

Ultimately, Patty's Strategic Foresight helped her create the conditions required for future success. She set herself up for a positive outcome by anticipating obstacles and opportunities, and she achieved it by making smart choices and taking intelligent action.

Yeah, but...

"I believe the mind is powerful and 'what you think about, you bring about.' Why would I want to think about everything that could go wrong? That will only attract bad things into my life."

You may be familiar with a philosophy popularly known as *the Law of Attraction*, which suggests that positive thoughts attract more positivity into your life while negative thoughts attract more negativity.

Strategic Foresight can sometimes spark resistance for people who faithfully practice the Law of Attraction because this skill involves turning your attention toward something other than exactly what you want. In the perfect Law of Attraction universe, we should only think about the good outcomes we want to create.

Personally, I don't think it's inherently negative to think about what might go wrong in a given situation. When done to the right extent and in the right way, it's just realistic. In fact, I wouldn't even label it as thinking about "bad" things. They're just things. Possibilities. Things that could happen that are less than ideal.

Ignoring the fact that these kinds of things can happen doesn't make them any *less* likely to happen. All it does is lull you into complacency and poor decisions. If you refuse to consider that a car accident is even possible, why bother wearing a seat belt?

Likewise, thinking about the less-than-ideal possibilities doesn't make them *more* likely to happen either. If you recognize that car accidents are possible and wear your seatbelt, you're not any more likely to get into a crash. You're just more likely to survive.

I too believe the mind is powerful. Positive thinking is a tool I rely on for dealing with life's inevitable challenges. That's why, when I consider those less-than-ideal things that could happen, I don't dwell in the problem. Instead, I leap quickly into finding a solution: *How can I prevent it? How can I prepare for it?* I use positive thinking to approach challenges and potential challenges with an optimistic can-do spirit.

Remember, being proactive isn't about living in fear of the future, and Strategic Foresight isn't about focusing on *everything* that can go wrong—that would be debilitating. It's just about acknowledging realistic possibilities, wearing your metaphorical seat belt, and trying your best to make it to your destination without a crash.

IN SUMMARY

Strategic Foresight is the driving force of proactivity. It is the skill that helps proactive professionals answer questions before they're even asked, address concerns before they're even expressed, and find solutions before anyone else even notices the problem. These people aren't magical, mystical beings. They're simply thinking ahead—using logic and imagination—and working backward to avoid obstacles, leverage opportunities, and create the best possible outcomes.

Of course, all of this would be futile without the next part of the proactive journey. After all, as Thomas Edison said, "Vision without execution is hallucination." So up next, we'll explore how to put all of this insight gained from the first four skills into action.

REFLECTION EXERCISES

1. Try to identify a time in the past when you successfully used Strategic Foresight to anticipate obstacles, opportunities, or

outcomes—even if you didn't realize it at the time. How did you do it, and what were the results? Did you use any of the strategies in this chapter (e.g., asking what if questions, identifying patterns, and so on), or did you do something different?

2. Are there certain situations where you look back and think, "I should have seen that coming"? If so, explore them with a sense of curiosity (not regret or self-pity) and try to recognize the signs you might have missed. What lessons can you learn for the future? How does this better prepare you to "see around corners"?

CHAPTER 9

INTENTIONAL ACTION

There are three types of people in this world: those who make things happen, those who watch things happen, and those who wonder what happened.

MARY KAY ASH, AMERICAN BUSINESSWOMAN (1918–2001)

THE FIFTH ESSENTIAL component of The Proactive Skillset is Intentional Action. This is defined as *the ability to initiate timely, deliberate action to create a desirable future state.*

At this point, we've come a long way on the proactive journey. Yet we haven't actually gotten anywhere. Until now, we've merely prepared for the journey. We've looked at our map and found our place on it; we've decided where we want to go and shone our light on the path ahead. But here is where the physical work begins. Without action, all of our efforts thus far are wasted.

It might surprise you that it's taken us this long to get here. After all, the word *act* is embedded in the word *proactive*. Action is an inherent part of it. Up until now, the skills we've discussed have all been cognitive. They have more to do with how you think rather than how you act. You've learned actions to take to help build these skills, but the skills themselves are merely thought processes.

Still, we couldn't have come to action any sooner. Without the first four skills, we have no way to ensure that the actions we take are any better or different than those of reactive people. (You'll notice that the word *act* is embedded in there too!) The skills we've learned to this point help prepare us for making the right choices regarding what actions to take.

When you look back at the book thus far, you'll notice that every example incorporates action in some way. In fact, here's a fun exercise: Grab your favorite pen or highlighter, and go back through every story of Proactive Patty and Reactive Rita. Underline or highlight the actions each took and try to identify the differences.

You'll probably notice that Rita, at times, failed to act at all. Her preference, we might assume, was to wait for absolute certainty. She was unwilling to take any risk in deciding how to act on her own. She wanted someone else to simply tell her or for circumstances to clearly direct her. When forced to act, Rita often did so impulsively without thinking through the consequences or what she hoped to achieve.

Patty, conversely, demonstrated Intentional Action in each scenario. So let's explore exactly what that means.

The definition for this skill has several key elements. First, it says we must *initiate*. This means "to begin." Reactive people wait to be told; proactive people simply start. We're able to do so intelligently because of the other skills in our proactive skillset.

It also says we're taking *timely*, *deliberate* action. Proactive people are swift and decisive, but their actions are based on thoughtful, conscious consideration. Reactive people impulsively do without thinking; proactive people think before doing, but that doesn't mean they're slow to act.

Finally, we do all of this to create a *desirable future state*. Once again, the other skills in The Proactive Skillset help us determine what that really means in any given situation.

It's important to note that, at times, *in*action can be a form of action. Consciously choosing *not* to act is a valid type of Intentional Action and is appropriate in some situations. However, proactive people are careful not to use that as an excuse. They have a bias toward action—when all things are equal, they choose to act.

CHOOSE YOUR OWN ADVENTURE

My love of reading started early. When I was a kid, I discovered Choose Your Own Adventure books and was immediately hooked.

For those of you who don't have the same fond memories of them, here's a quick explanation. As the reader, you assume the role of the main character. The book starts by establishing a basic premise, like finding a time machine or embarking on an undersea voyage.

Then, right when the story hits a crucial point, it presents two (or more!) options. Do you investigate that mysterious noise or retreat back to your spaceship? Do you talk to the creepy groundskeeper or keep exploring the haunted house?

You, dear reader, get to decide which way you want to go. Over and over again, you do this, and your decisions shape the story.

I remember reaching the end of each Choose Your Own Adventure book and promptly turning back to the beginning. Simply by making different choices, you could create dozens of different stories, each wildly different from the next.

What does this have to do with proactivity and Intentional Action? Well, in my view, life is like a Choose Your Own Adventure book. You are the main character. Your story unfolds based on the choices you make and the actions you take. At any point in time, you have options, each of which may lead you in a different direction. Thankfully, you have The Proactive Skillset to help you in the decision-making process. But ultimately, *you* are responsible for the story you create. Unfortunately, you can't flip back to the beginning to create another one.

Intentional Action is about taking ownership over your actions, not relying on others to tell you what to do or do it for you. It's about taking intelligent, calculated risks, and, most importantly, it's about using your good judgment to move the adventure forward in any way you choose.

FACING THE ENEMY

Taking action doesn't sound difficult on its surface. After all, everyone takes action—in some form or another—every day. Yet Intentional Action is hard for reactive people. I've found the reason is a common enemy: *fear*.

Reactive people are afraid of taking the wrong action, and they're afraid of facing the unknown consequences of action. As a result, they procrastinate and abdicate responsibility to others.

Taking action is risky, no doubt. It requires putting yourself "out there" so to speak. Action is noticeable, and it's yours to own, whatever the results. But proactive people account for this risk, relying on The Proactive Skillset to help manage and minimize it.

Reactive people don't know it, but they actually create *more* risk through their lack of action. It might feel safer in the moment, but later, once the future unfolds upon them, their error is clear to those who are looking.

Reactive people also create greater risk through their uncalculated actions. Fear pushes them into rash decisions, and their impulsive actions increase the likelihood of danger ahead. Thus they encounter more fear in the future, and the cycle continues.

Embracing Intentional Action means facing the inevitable fear it produces and the grim reality of the alternative. Yes, it comes with a certain amount of risk, but it's far outweighed by the potential rewards. And the risk itself is negligible when compared with the risks of reactivity.

DEVELOPING INTENTIONAL ACTION

While all the skills in The Proactive Skillset are important, this one is particularly so. For many, developing the skill of Intentional Action is the most challenging part of becoming proactive. It's where the prover-bial rubber meets the road. The following strategies will help ease the process.

TAKE INITIATIVE (WITHOUT OVERSTEPPING)

When I tell people to take initiative in the workplace, they often express concern. They don't want to step on toes or get in trouble for crossing some invisible line. I get it—some people have had bad experiences. They've been micromanaged into a permanent state of reactivity. Others have simply overstepped in the past and are scared to try again.

To be clear, "taking initiative" isn't simply a green light to do what you want, when you want. It's something that carries risk and, when not done properly, can create problems. But it's also not that complicated.

Despite what you may have heard, it's not always about asking permis-sion versus begging forgiveness. Much of the time, Victor Hugo's famous quote covers it: "Initiative is doing the right thing without being told."

Here's the basic rule for taking initiative: *If you know what needs to be done and you know it's something within the scope of your position and capabili-ties, do it.* Don't wait for direction. Don't look for approval. Don't hand it off to someone else. Take Intentional Action. No permission or forgiveness is needed. If you're qualified by virtue of your job and your abilities, there's no reason to question yourself.

If something falls clearly *outside* of the scope of your position and capa-bilities, that's a different story, and this is where initiative can go awry. I'm not advocating insubordination here. The workplace has a chain of com-mand for a reason. Ignoring it may cause all kinds of unintended conse-quences. Recognize the limits of your authority and respect the hierarchy of your organization.

When you're just learning to take Intentional Action, you may realize in some instances that you're not quite sure where those boundaries are. You think you know what needs to be done, but you don't know if it's within the scope of your position. Perhaps it's not specifically spelled out in your job description, but it makes sense for you to handle it. Do you take initiative or do you hold back?

Unfortunately, there are no hard-and-fast rules for how to handle such situations. You have to use your best judgment based on what you know about your role and your workplace. Does your manager prefer to see people make decisions and take action on their own, even if they occasionally miss the mark? Or is your manager the hands-on type who wants to have input beforehand?

If you don't know the answer to these questions, have a proactive conversation with your manager. Get clear guidance regarding where those invisible lines are for the future. And if they're unnecessarily restrictive, ask what needs to be done to loosen them.

In any case, before taking initiative, always ensure you've done your due diligence. Use the other skills in your proactive skillset to verify that the action you're considering is reasonable and defensible. If someone asks why you took a particular action, will you be able to offer a logical, well-thought-out explanation? If not, taking initiative is not worth the risk.

Even under the best of circumstances, you may occasionally still miss the mark. You might have been trying to take initiative, but you realize in hindsight that you made a mistake. We'll discuss this more in the next chapter, but, for now, recognize that it's an almost inevitable part of the process. Presuming you've followed the guidelines here, you can recover from almost any honest mistake of overenthusiastic initiative.

FIND THE SPACE BETWEEN STIMULUS AND RESPONSE

Steven Covey, author of *The 7 Habits of Highly Effective People*, once said, "The key to being proactive is remembering that between stimulus and response there is space. That space represents our choice—how we will choose to respond to any given situation, person, thought, or event."

Finding that space is indeed the key to Intentional Action. In order to act with intention, you must first pause and think and then make your choice. This is where so many reactive people fall short. They allow the pressure of the moment to push them into careless choices and thoughtless action.

Being proactive is about acting consciously and with purpose. Within the context of a busy workplace, this can be difficult. Circumstances change in the blink of an eye, and you're expected to make split-second decisions. The idea of pausing to think before taking action may sound impossible, but I assure you: it's not. Remember that the use of a precious moment now could save many more in the future.

This is easier said than done, I know, especially when others are breathing down your neck for answers and action. But pausing doesn't require extraordinary amounts of time, and often, we have more time available than we think. We must simply choose to use it. Most people, you'll find, will be very understanding as well—as long as you tell them what you're doing. A simple statement like "I need a minute to think this through" will usually suffice.

BE RESOURCEFUL

Proactive people aren't afraid of using their resources to figure things out on their own. They take Intentional Action to answer their own questions and find their own solutions, rather than pushing that action onto others.

See if this scenario sounds familiar...

Reactive Rita has a question about how to complete a certain process. She sends an email to her helpful colleague, Henry, and waits. She's at a standstill with this task until Henry answers her question, but still Rita waits, wasting valuable time for herself and others. When Henry finally responds, his answer is a little confusing, so Rita seeks clarification with another email. And again, she waits.

Whether this kind of thing is driven by fear or laziness, it's a purely reactive behavior. Rita immediately taps Henry for her answer but fails to use any of the other resources at her disposal. People are, indeed, one type of resource. But their time is limited. Your colleagues may be happy to answer questions when needed, but they also have a job to do. And in most cases, you have other resources available.

Proactive Patty would never do what Rita did. Patty respects Henry's time and doesn't want to impose on him unless it's really needed. Plus, she understands the value of finding answers on her own. She'd rather spend some energy searching through procedures manuals and using trial and error to figure it out. By doing this, she knows she'll be more capable of answering other questions that pop up in the future. If and when she needs help from Henry or anyone else, she'll also be more informed. She'll be able to discuss what she found on her own and can request the specific assistance she needs to fill in the gaps.

In today's world, we have the largest source of information ever available in the history of humankind at our fingertips. Yet, all too often, I encounter so-called professionals who fail to use the Internet to answer even the most basic questions.

I used to hold free monthly training webinars for my ten-thousand-plus newsletter subscribers from around the world. It was virtually guaranteed that every time I sent out an invitation publicizing the time of the event (in both US Eastern and Pacific times), I would get a response from someone in another part of the country or world asking, "What time would that be for me?"

I was absolutely stunned when this first started happening. Why were these people asking me? The question, essentially, pushed their required action onto me. I had to Google the answer for them and then respond to their email when they could have just as easily done it for themselves. Finally, I started proactively including a link to the world time zone converter in my webinar invitations.

By then, the stark reality had hit me: some people would just rather have other people tell them the answers, even when Google is faster and easier.

I recently received another email from a website visitor who was looking for an e-book I wrote several years ago. Because the rights for the book were sold to another company, it's not available on my website, and this person wanted to know where she could get it. She knew the name of the book. She knew my name (the author). Had she typed this information into Google, the first result would have been the book. In fact, the first three results would have provided her with an answer immediately. But instead she emailed me and then sat around, waiting for a response—when the answer was literally at her fingertips if only she had been resourceful.

If it feels like I'm belaboring the point, I probably am out of sheer frustration. Don't place unnecessary burdens on others. You have resources, not only online but within your organization. Use them to answer your own questions and solve your own problems. Use people as your last resort or when no other resource will do.

THINK "PROGRESS, NOT PERFECTION"

Intentional Action is supposed to help you create a desirable future state. However, it's important to remember that this usually happens incrementally. It's not about taking one perfect action that will catapult you to your final destination. *It's better to take one small action today rather than wait for some imagined perfect action you could take tomorrow.*

As Edmund Burke so eloquently said, "Nobody made a greater mistake than he who did nothing because he could do only little."

Unrealistic expectations make it easy to procrastinate. If the goal is perfection, you'll likely never feel ready to take action. Instead, aim for action that creates *progress*. Even microscopic movements are valuable if you're headed in the right direction.

Yeah, but...

"The pace of my job is insane, so I rely on my instinct to tell me what to do. I don't have time to pause and think about things. In fact, I actually do better just *off the cuff.*"

The strategy of "pausing" to think before taking action is how we learn to be intentional. When people are stuck in reactivity, they rely solely on instinct. As a result, their actions are often unintentional and based in fear.

However, with experience and practice, you can develop a proactive instinct—a kind of sixth sense that tells you the right action to take with little conscious deliberation. In the Stages of Competence model (presented in chapter 3), this is the final stage, unconscious competence. It's the pinnacle of mastery and a place most people aspire to reach.

If you're currently relying on instinct, I'll quote Dr. Phil and ask, "How's that working out for you?" If you're proactively preventing avoidable problems and minimizing the damage of unavoidable ones, your instinct is serving you well. However, if you're still encountering some of the telltale signs of reactivity, your instinct is leading you astray.

Only you can determine how it's working—*but you have to be honest.*

This discussion reminds me a little of those people who procrastinate and then say they do their best work when under tremendous time pressure. Is it true? Maybe. Or maybe it's just a convenient excuse for bad behavior. Maybe they'd do even better without the time pressure.

Most people benefit from taking a little time to make their choices and actions conscious and intentional. You may be different. Maybe "off the cuff" works for you. But don't convince yourself of that if the evidence isn't really there.

As for the time factor, I get it. Work is insane, and you have to move fast. Pausing requires the luxury of time, which we don't always have. But don't impose time pressures that aren't really there. Even in the most chaotic workplaces, a moment can (usually) be spared.

IN SUMMARY

Imagine standing in the middle of a football field while an NFL game happens around you.

"Don't worry!" you shout to the coach. "I'll just watch from here."

"*What?*" cries Coach. "If you're on the field, you better play!"

"Oh fine," you say reluctantly. "I'll catch the ball if it comes to me."

"Are you kidding?" Coach is obviously worried at this point.

"OK," you finally agree. "Tell me what to do, and I'll do it."

At this point, Coach is staring at you, aghast.

"Get off the field," he finally says. "You're gonna hurt yourself."

Action is what separates participants from spectators. I enjoy watching football on TV, but I don't really want to play. I'd rather stay on my couch, eat chips, and let the tough guys do the hard part. I am thankful that's my choice.

But at work, you're in the game whether you like it or not. Simply by virtue of being employed, you're a player on the field. Sure, you can choose to stand there, waiting for the ball to come to you and letting others call the shots. But eventually you're just going to get in the way. If you're not an active participant, it's best to get off the field.

My football analogy is harsh but apt. No one wants a player who can't pull his or her weight. Others are relying on you to do your part. Your coach (i.e., your manager) is there to help, but you already know how to play the game. You're a pro, and you belong on the field. Have confidence in your abilities.

Intentional Action is how we make progress on our goals and ultimately reach them.

Still, you can't win every game. Even the best players fumble from time to time. In the next chapter, we'll talk about why that's perfectly OK—and even beneficial when done right.

⌒

REFLECTION EXERCISES

1. Identify a time in the past when you either showed too much initiative (and overstepped) or too little (and underperformed) and it came back to bite you. What compelled you to act the way you did? What does this experience teach you about using initiative appropriately?

2. Reflect on your ability to act with intention. What makes it difficult? Consider both external barriers (such as workplace politics or time pressures) and internal ones (such as fear). Are these barriers real or imagined? What can you do to manage and minimize them to free yourself?

CHAPTER 10

SELF-EVALUATION

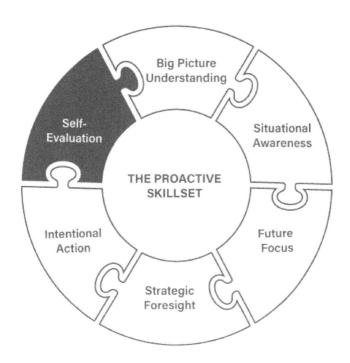

By stopping regularly to look inward...I stay connected to the source of my actions and thoughts and can guide them with considerably more intention.

DUSTIN MOSKOVITZ, AMERICAN ENTREPRENEUR (BORN IN 1984)

THE SIXTH AND "final" essential component of The Proactive Skillset is Self-Evaluation. This is defined as *the ability to critically assess your behaviors and results and make appropriate adjustments to enhance future outcomes.*

Ah, we finally made it! We're on the last leg of our proactive journey. But don't forget what I told you before: this is a journey that never truly ends. Everything we discover here will serve to prepare us for the ongoing journey ahead.

In this part of the process, we take stock of where we are and how we got here and make sure we're on the right track. After all, we're using a map of our own creation. And while we've certainly done our best to choose the right path and avoid obstacles, there's always a chance that we've miscalculated somewhere along the way or accidentally veered off in the wrong direction. It's time to course-correct if so.

Throughout this book, you've learned what's possible with proactivity. With a little effort, you can better manage problems—sidestep them altogether or at least minimize their impact. You can set yourself up for success in the future by taking the right steps today.

Unfortunately, things don't always go perfectly according to plan. Sometimes, our best proactive intentions go awry. We encounter circumstances we never saw coming, or we inadvertently create problems instead of preventing them.

When these things happen, we face an opportunity for growth. Instead of beating ourselves up, we can leverage the skill of Self-Evaluation to learn from the experience and expand our proactive skillset.

Let's explore the definition of this skill in detail.

The term *critically assess* means *to appraise with a critical eye*. That doesn't mean you're focused solely on negative criticism; you're merely seeking truth, acknowledging what's working and what's not.

With this skill, you're using honest analysis to critique your own *behaviors and results*. Understanding the connection between these two things and taking responsibility for them is the foundation of proactivity. Your ability to impartially look at what you've created allows you to better appreciate your power.

Ultimately, you can use this knowledge to *make appropriate adjustments*. After all, no one is perfect; we can't predict or control every possible eventuality. We have to be willing and able to adapt and flex our proactivity muscles as new situations arise and more information becomes available.

We modify our choices and actions moving forward in an effort to *enhance future outcomes*. The goal is always to create a better tomorrow for ourselves and others.

This process is especially exciting because everything we learn feeds back into our Big Picture Understanding. It helps refine and improve our map. It's a repeating cycle that allows us to continually build our proactive skillset through practice and experience.

IMPERFECT PROACTIVITY

In truth, being proactive is often a thankless job. As former US Congressman Barney Frank once said, "You don't really get credit for crisis averted." At the time, he was referring to the financial collapse of 2008 and acknowledging that, while things were bad, they could have been a lot worse if not for some proactive measures. But it's hard to prove a negative and even harder to take credit for something that *didn't* happen.

When we're successfully proactive, we encounter fewer, smaller problems. We feel more in control of our circumstances. As the subtitle of this book suggests, being proactive means we're not only on top of things but we're actually getting ahead of them.

Success, in this respect, is difficult to accurately assess. So many factors are at play—some within our control, some outside of it. Sometimes, we can do everything right and still end up with unfavorable outcomes. That's simply the nature of life.

Proactivity is an imperfect science and a subjective art.

Difficult though it may be, it's still important to note our successes and failures, to look at what happened, what we did and why, and evaluate how it turned out.

When we fail to predict approaching problems, for example, we need to go back in time mentally and look for any telltale signs we might have missed. When we take action, but it doesn't yield the results we were hoping for, we need to pause and figure out what we could have done differently. When we take initiative but accidentally overstep, we need to clearly define the boundary we crossed and figure out how to prevent it from happening again.

These challenges are not uncommon. Used intelligently, they can provide us with valuable information for the future, expanding our Big Picture Understanding of workplace norms, problem solving, decision making, and the broader skill of proactivity itself.

At the same time, we also need to acknowledge when all goes well—when we take the right action at the right time to create the favorable outcome we were seeking. These are precious learning experiences too.

Such situations confirm our Big Picture Understanding and help boost confidence in our abilities.

THE GROWTH CYCLE

Like learning how to be proactive, the process of personal growth is continuous too. As a trainer, I am deeply passionate about it, and I'm always surprised when I meet people who aren't. After all, isn't growth what life is all about?

Yet, on a semiregular basis, I seem to encounter people who almost have *contempt* for it. When a company hires me to conduct training sessions for their employees, there's usually one person (at least) who doesn't want to be there. I can always recognize this person clearly by watching body language. He or she will lean back in the chair, arms folded across the chest, and watch me like I'm some kind of dancing monkey—a rare specimen that is simultaneously entertaining, annoying, and confusing.

I can proudly say that, most of the time, I can bring these people around. In fact, I consider it a special talent. Inevitably, people will let their guard down just enough to really hear what I'm saying, and that's when things shift. They sit up straighter, take notes, and actually begin to learn.

These people start off with a mindset of unwillingness because they truly believe there's nothing I can teach them. Many of them are very good at what they do. As a result, they've stopped growing. They've come to think that learning is no longer required, and that's a dangerous proposition.

Here's my take on it: *There is no such thing as "standing still" in the workplace. You're either moving forward or you're falling behind. That's the choice.*

"Moving forward" doesn't mean you're always getting promoted or climbing some invisible ladder. It just means you're growing.

No one stays "on top of their game" without fighting to stay there. Once you think you know everything, something new will come along and knock you off that pedestal. A new technology, a new process, or a new plan for the future will appear. You'll be a beginner again. If you close yourself off to the new things, you'll eventually become obsolete.

The growth cycle requires four never-ending steps: Reflect → Learn → Adjust → Grow.

It's that simple. Reflect on the situation you're in, learn from it, adjust your approach in the future, and this is what creates growth. Growth is what keeps you from making the same missteps over and over again. Growth is what helps you create better results time after time.

No matter where you are in your career or what you're doing on any given day, a growth-oriented individual will always be in some stage of the growth cycle. When you're not, you've stopped moving forward, and you've started falling behind.

THE STRETCH ZONE

I understand why some people resist the idea of growth. It's uncomfortable. Self-Evaluation is the underlying requirement for growth, and it can be downright terrifying sometimes. It's only natural to shy away from things that make us squirmy.

You've probably heard of the *comfort zone*. It's a popular term because people intuitively understand what it means. They get it because it's so unequivocally *normal*.

The following illustration summarizes what I've learned about the comfort zone.

FIGURE 5. THE ZONES OF COMFORT/DISCOMFORT

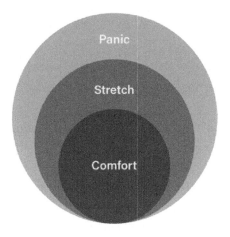

Depending on who you are and what life has thrown your way, perhaps you're quite familiar with the comfort zone. It's that cozy place where everything is easy and nothing risky happens. Of course, nothing especially great happens there either.

Just outside the comfort zone, you'll find the stretch zone. This is the place where you're a little uncomfortable; you're stretching yourself in new and different ways, but you're still able to manage. It's not easy, but it's not impossibly hard either.

Stray too far out in this direction and you'll eventually hit the panic zone, where all hell breaks loose. This is what most people are afraid of. Once you've hit the panic zone, you're so far outside of the comfort zone, you're likely to end up frozen in fear. There's nothing left to do at that point but pray.

The stretch zone is a good place to be. Proactive people spend most of their time there. Sure, it's not as safe as the comfort zone, but it offers much more in the way of rewards. It's challenging, even thrilling at times, to see what's possible in the stretch zone. It takes more effort, and it involves more risk, but it's how growth happens.

And here's the most interesting part: *The more time you spend in the stretch zone, the bigger your comfort zone actually gets. In essence, you become comfortable being uncomfortable.*

That's pretty cool. It means that, with practice, growth can get easier. Self-Evaluation could even become fun.

Reactive people tend to camp out in the comfort zone. They roll out their snug sack and hunker down. When life inevitably invades, they reluctantly venture out—most often they head straight for the panic zone—and then scurry back in as quickly as possible.

In order to truly excel at something, be it proactivity or anything else, we can't be afraid of a little discomfort.

Honest Self-Evaluation and true growth *should* take you out of the comfort zone. You know you're doing it right when it makes you feel a little squirmy. But the more you do it, the more comfortable it will become.

DEVELOPING SELF-EVALUATION

The skill of Self-Evaluation requires both humility and confidence. On the surface, these two traits might appear to be at odds with one another. How can one be *authentically* humble and confident at the same time without also looking schizophrenic? This concern can be remedied by exploring the meaning of these two words.

For our purposes, *humility* is simply the ability to look at yourself honestly and see exactly what's there—the good, the bad, and the ugly. It's about being willing to acknowledge your faults, weaknesses, and areas for improvement. It requires setting aside ego and admitting your own imperfections.

Confidence, as it's used here, simply refers to the willingness to improve. It means knowing you're capable of doing better and believing you have the power to grow.

If you're humble enough to be honest with yourself and confident enough to make changes when needed, you're already halfway there.

But that's not all you need. The following strategies will help you hone your Self-Evaluation skills and round out your proactive skillset.

FIX MISTAKES

By now, you're probably getting sick of Proactive Patty. Maybe you're even feeling a little resentful toward her, wondering how it is that everything always works out just so for Perfect Patty. Let me assure you, Patty is only human, and she too makes mistakes.

Here's a scenario that should make you feel a little better about Patty.

> While adding some finishing touches to a presentation for her boss, Patty notices a rather prominent and frequently repeated error in the work. A certain product specification has been listed incorrectly.
>
> Proactive as ever, Patty decides to fix it, even though her boss didn't specifically ask for this kind of assistance. She sends the final spruced-up presentation back to her boss along with a quick note informing him of the correction she made.
>
> Moments later, her boss responds to her email with a terse message of his own.

"That wasn't an error, Patty. The specs on this product are changing. Please correct your corrections."

Ouch.

Unfortunately, Patty was relying on an inaccurate understanding of the situation. She didn't have all of the information but presumed she did. She made what appeared to be a logical leap, yet she was just plain wrong. Her actions might have been helpful *if* she had been working with the right set of facts. But sadly, she didn't know what she didn't know, and she inadvertently created more work for herself.

I have a confession to make. In this scenario, I am Proactive Patty. Yes, dear reader, I am guilty as charged. I did (proactively) warn you that I'm not perfect, didn't I? Well, here's your proof.

So let me tell you how I handled it.

I fixed the mistake, *quickly*, and then jumped into the growth cycle. I reflected on what happened, learned from it, adjusted my behavior, and grew as a result.

Equally important: I shared the lesson with my boss. I didn't make excuses or try to defend my mistake. He knew I was trying to help. I just told him it wouldn't happen again. Next time, I said, if I found something that might be incorrect, I'd bring it to his attention first. He appreciated this, though, at the same time, he encouraged me to continue proactively fixing his many irrefutable errors of grammar and spelling.

I'd be lying if I said this was a fun experience. I was embarrassed and frustrated with myself. I've never forgotten it. But ultimately it made me a better proactive professional. It showed me the limits of my knowledge—something I've (humbly) had to remind myself of through the years. It also showed me how to (confidently) recover from errors of judgment.

These things happen, and something similar may happen to you at some point. The worst response is to throw your hands in the air and decide you'll never again try to be proactive. That's not the solution.

Fix your mistakes immediately, define your strategy for ensuring it never happens again, and share that strategy with the people who need it. Then, make sure you follow through. Nothing is more counterproductive than repeatedly making the same mistakes. Albert Einstein once said, "Insanity is doing the same thing over and over again and expecting different results."

Please, be *sanely* proactive.

SEEK FEEDBACK

When it comes to seeing reality, we're all working with a limited point of view. We see the world from our own unique perspective, which is great most of the time. However, where Self-Evaluation is concerned, our ability to truly see ourselves is quite narrow.

Think about it this way: When you look in a mirror, you're only able to see the front side of yourself, right? If you want to know how your butt looks in those new jeans, you can swivel and turn and twist, but you'll never get an accurate view. If you really want to know, you need to ask someone else. Most of the time, you find someone whose opinion matters and hopefully someone you trust to tell you the truth.

The same rules apply in the workplace. You should certainly hold up a figurative mirror and look at yourself, but recognize that the picture is incomplete. In order to see what you can't see in yourself, you need to get feedback from others.

Whose feedback really matters depends on your situation, but I'd venture to guess your boss's opinion is pretty important. However, you may also want to seek feedback from other trusted colleagues who you know will be honest, supportive, and informed enough to offer helpful insight.

Feedback falls into two broad categories.

1. **Direct Feedback**—This happens when someone tells you in specific terms what you need to know.

Reactive people often wait for direct feedback to come to them. Unfortunately, in most workplaces, feedback isn't offered as frequently (or as directly) as it should be. It's nice when it falls into your lap, but it's not always that easy.

You can proactively solicit direct feedback by making a direct inquiry. Whenever possible, be specific about what you want to know. Asking your boss, "How am I doing?" is far too broad to provide meaningful information. Instead ask your boss, "What do you think of my strategy on the ABC project? Are there changes or improvements you would recommend?"

2. **Indirect Feedback**—This happens when you gather clues and interpret them to determine what you need to know.

Sometimes you can figure out what's working and what's not simply by monitoring the environment. However, indirect feedback is tricky because it leaves much to the imagination and thus isn't always accurate.

If your boss is clearly displeased with an action you took, you can deduce that something went wrong. Retracing your steps, you may be able to figure it out on your own. But be cautious. Misinterpreting signals can compound the problem.

When in doubt, seek direct feedback. Clear communication helps ensure the message doesn't get corrupted.

Feedback helps you understand when you're off track so you can change course if needed. But remember that the bigger goal of feedback (and Self-Evaluation in general) is to inform your Big Picture Understanding— to use the information in the future to make better decisions and take more effective action. Always ask yourself:

- What does this teach me?
- What will I do differently with this new information?
- What kinds of situations does this lesson apply to?

Yeah, but...

"When I reflect on my performance at work, I'm struck by how little I control. When things go well, I don't deserve the credit. And when things go poorly, I don't deserve the blame."

There's a reason the serenity prayer is one of the most frequently repeated prayers on earth. I'm sure you've heard it before, but just in case you need a refresher, here it is:

"God grant me the serenity to accept the things I cannot change, the courage to change the things I can, and the wisdom to know the difference."[4]

Whether or not you're religious, almost anyone can appreciate the sentiment. That last part is especially important

---

4   Reinhold Niebuhr, American theologian

because everything else relies on it. If you aren't wise enough to know the difference between what's within your control and what's not, all the serenity and courage in the world won't do you any good.

Of course, to complicate matters, control isn't a simple black-and-white question. There are different shades of control. The only thing you completely control is yourself—your choices, actions, thoughts, feelings, and responses. But beyond that, you also have influence over a great many things.

I once coached an executive assistant (we'll call her Ashley) who felt constantly at the mercy of her boss's every whim. Ashley had fully released control over her time and work. She was living in reactivity and was miserable.

A little honest Self-Evaluation helped Ashley see the areas where she *did* have control (over herself) and influence (over her boss). She saw that it was her responsibility to help set reasonable expectations, for example. She couldn't change the fact that her boss would interrupt her all day long—that was part of the job—but she *could* change how she managed his constant stream of demands.

Once Ashley started using her power, the entire dynamic changed. Her boss actually came to view her as a strategic partner, not just a dumping ground for to-do items. By proactively managing priorities, she was able to steer herself and her boss where they wanted to go. Both of them were happier and more productive as a result.

I challenge you to reassess your areas of control and influence. Are you defaulting to a place of no control because it allows you to comfortably deny your own responsibility? Are you refusing to see where credit (or blame) is rightfully deserved?

When things are truly beyond the scope of your control and influence, it's useful to acknowledge it but then shift attention back to yourself—your response and next actions. These things are *always* fully in your control. Don't discount your power and don't abdicate your responsibility.

IN SUMMARY

Personally, I've always been a fan of Self-Evaluation, but that doesn't mean I always enjoy doing it.

Here's something important I learned not too long ago: Those times when I resist Self-Evaluation? Those are the times I really need it. In my experience, Self-Evaluation is hardest when I know there's something I need to change or improve, which is often, yet I don't want to face it. Being a growth-oriented individual, this means I find myself, at times, resisting the very thing I need most.

As I write, I'm struck by how obvious this idea is. Of course, we all resist acknowledging our weaknesses to some extent. As humans, we're evolutionarily hardwired to resist it. Showing weakness can threaten our survival. Our cave dwelling ancestors surely knew that.

But in today's world, that instinct is misplaced. Our survival, in the modern workplace jungle, is very much *enhanced* by Self-Evaluation. Why? Because it helps us create a more detailed, accurate, and useful map for the future. It is the critical link between who we are today and what we're capable of tomorrow.

REFLECTION EXERCISES

1. Reflect on an average week at work. What percentage of the time do you spend in the comfort zone versus in the stretch zone? In the upcoming week, what will you do to increase your time in the stretch zone?

2. Identify a time in the past when you experienced the growth cycle. Clarify exactly what happened, what you learned, how you adjusted your behavior, and the growth you experienced as a result. Do you believe this process is possible in *any* situation?

PART 3

CONCLUSION

CHAPTER 11

MORE PROACTIVE PRACTICES

THROUGHOUT THIS BOOK, you've learned about The Proactive Skillset, a group of tools designed to help you think, act, and be proactive. By mastering this skillset and applying the tools in the workplace, you *will* become the proactive professional.

By now, I'm confident you understand the theory of proactivity. I hope you've also gained a wide variety of practical application strategies as demonstrated in the many examples. For the majority of our time together, we've focused on using The Proactive Skillset in managing your work and getting things done. This is the general area where most people expect to reap the greatest return from being proactive.

However, I firmly believe that being proactive has the potential to enhance all areas of your work life (and life in general). That's why I'm using this chapter to highlight some additional proactive practices—specific things *anyone* can do, starting now—that apply to two particularly important activities: managing relationships and managing your career.

Your ability to manage these two things can deeply impact your chances of achieving long-term professional success and, more importantly, life happiness. Yet few people take a proactive role in their relationships or their career. Such things are often neglected until (you guessed it) things go wrong.

The tips in this chapter are meant to encourage you to proactively *design* the relationships and career you want. It is my hope that this chapter will inspire you to think more about how to use your new proactive skillset in all areas of work and life.

PROACTIVE RELATIONSHIP MANAGEMENT

BE INTENTIONAL

Many people enter into working relationships with a haphazard, re-active attitude. They don't think about the relationship they want to create; they invest very little time, energy, and effort into it. They simply allow their relationships to happen. Later, they look back and wonder how things got so dysfunctional.

If you were to ask any happily married couple how they created a success-ful partnership, most would say it took some serious work. Perhaps you've experienced this firsthand in your personal life. Professional partnerships are no different. If you don't first know what success looks like, you're at a real disadvantage from the beginning. If you don't intentionally work at it, you'll just have to take your chances with what you get.

ARTICULATE NEEDS

I've said (somewhat facetiously) that being proactive can make you prac-tically clairvoyant. Trust me; your boss will love it. But unfortunately, you can't expect others to read your mind.

When you need something, you can wait for people to figure it out on their own—which could take a very, very long time—or you can simply speak up. Reactive people stay silent, hoping that others will pick up on their signals or magically put the pieces together correctly. They tentatively dance around important topics and often get stepped on in the process. Proactive people state their needs clearly. They aren't afraid of standing up for themselves and establishing their power in the relationship.

CLARIFY AVAILABILITY

In the working world, people are busy, and communication is often strained because of limited time availability. People launch into important discussions only to abruptly stop when they realize they're late for their next meeting. Others routinely interrupt their unsuspecting colleagues without bothering to ask if it's a good time to talk.

Prevent these problems by clarifying availability for yourself and others before engaging in in-depth conversations. For example, "Do you have fifteen minutes to review these numbers with me?" or "I only have five minutes right now; let's set up a time for later."

It may indeed make more sense to schedule the conversation for another time, when both people can give it their undivided attention. In other situations, you may opt to go ahead and squeeze it in, with the understanding that time is short and further discussion should be saved for later.

In any case, you've proactively done your best to make communication convenient for everyone. You've also set yourself up for a more productive conversation by defining time restraints up front and helping ensure everyone involved can devote attention to it.

MEET CONSISTENTLY

Meetings in the workplace are important because they provide an opportunity for real-time communication. Whether they happen face to face or over the phone, they still offer enormous value for building, maintaining, and strengthening partnerships.

Unfortunately, many people discount the importance of meeting regularly. They're only motivated enough to meet with their key workplace partners when something isn't working and they need to address it. This is reactive relationship management.

I recommend meeting consistently with important partners, like your boss, even when problems *don't* exist. Doing so allows you to gather informal feedback on a regular basis. It also encourages both parties to raise important issues before they become urgent (Q2 items in the Time Management Matrix—see chapter 7). Finally, devoting regular time to the relationship helps deepen rapport, making it easier to discuss and resolve issues when they inevitably do arise.

Schedule a routine time to get together at intervals that make sense for your workplace and working relationship. That might mean weekly, monthly, or even daily in some cases. And don't be tempted to cancel the meeting if there's "nothing" to talk about. There's *always* something.

PROACTIVE CUSTOMER SERVICE

TAKE THE LEAD

When interacting directly with customers, whether internal or external, you play the role of expert. Your job is to lead the conversation to ensure the customer's needs are met. Remember that customers don't know what information you need from them or what questions they should be asking. You do.

That doesn't mean you should attempt to *control* the conversation but rather *guide* it gracefully by asking the appropriate questions, listening, and sharing helpful information. You have (more than likely) experienced similar conversations numerous times before. You probably handle the same inquiries and resolve the same problems from customers week after week. That doesn't mean you can cut them off and jump to conclusions about what they need. But it does mean you can offer a special insight they don't have.

Don't wait for the customer to tell you how to do your job.

Note: you'll find an example of reactive versus proactive customer service in the appendix.

EXPLAIN AND SET EXPECTATIONS

Customers don't know what you're doing when there's a long silent pause on the phone. They don't know what you're up to when your fingers are furiously tap-tap-tapping on the keyboard and your eyes are feverishly searching the computer screen. They don't need to know all the details, but they do need some reassurance. Otherwise, the natural inclination is to worry. Too many people have had bad service experiences.

You can proactively put your customer's mind at ease by simply explaining what's happening and setting expectations early. For example, "You might hear a few minutes of silence while I review your account," or "I'm taking a few notes as you speak so there might be a short pause in the conversation."

This is especially important when the customer can't see you. However, in person, it's still a useful strategy. This is why some companies require their new hires to wear pins that say, "Please be patient. I'm in training." It's a proactive way of telling the customer what's going on and what to expect.

The more you can prepare your customers up front and keep them informed along the way, the better things will go. This rule applies to *every* customer interaction, regardless of your industry or role.

PROACTIVE SALES

THINK LONG TERM

All sales professionals know the basic stats of the gig. They can tell you how many "touches" it takes to turn a lead into a sale, how much more likely a customer is to buy again once they're already a customer, and the fact that, no matter what, you'll always lose a certain portion of your customer base each year. The realities of the job are no secret, yet reactivity runs rampant in the sales world.

Proactive sales professionals take a long-term perspective. They recognize that nurturing a lead today might not pay incredible dividends tomorrow, but it could two years from now. They never sacrifice a happy future customer for a quick buck today. They would rather make sure their customers get exactly what they want and need, even if it takes a long time to figure that out. Proactive professionals know that time isn't wasted. They're slowly building a fan club—a ruthlessly loyal customer and referral base that will make their job easier with each passing day.

ASK, "WHAT ELSE?"

Proactive salespeople never sit on their laurels. They're always prospecting—even when they've just wrapped up a sale. They're always thinking about the next step, wondering what else they can do to help solve more of the customer's problems. Any big sale inevitably brings the temptation to slow down—after all, you deserve it! Look what you just accomplished! But proactive salespeople are vigilant about staying on course. They never let up.

PROACTIVE CAREER MANAGEMENT

COLLECT CAREER CURRENCY

Your professional accomplishments are like *career currency*. They get banked and add up, and over time, they are what earn you rewards in the future, such as promotions, bonuses, raises, and more opportunities. They elevate your visibility and reputation. Accomplishments are the most valuable things you can accumulate in the workplace.

Simply put, a *professional accomplishment* is anything that adds value to your team or organization.

No matter where you are currently in your career or where you want to go, nothing will serve you better than to focus on creating a wide array of impressive accomplishments. Take note of them when you do. Write them down so you don't forget the details in the future. If possible, identify the measurable outcomes you achieved.

The more career currency you collect now, the more leverage you will have in the future.

KEEP YOUR RÉSUMÉ UP-TO-DATE

You never know exactly when you'll find yourself back in the job market. Unfortunately, downsizing happens, and anyone (yes, *anyone*) can be a victim of layoffs. Sometimes you can see it coming; sometimes you simply can't. As one of my favorite career experts J.T. O'Donnell says, "Every job is temporary." This is an honest, though perhaps grim, perspective.

If (or when) an unexpected career shake-up happens to you, it's easy to imagine the stress you might feel. I've worked with *many* professionals who have gone through this; I know there are dozens of anxiety-inducing concerns that literally appear in the blink of an eye.

Updating your résumé is one concern you can alleviate proactively by keeping it current at all times. You don't want to waste time working on it when you're desperately in need of a new job. You won't do your best work, and it will only add to your stress.

Don't let your résumé get dusty! Review it at least once per quarter, add new accomplishments, and ensure it still accurately reflects who you are and what you want. If anything unexpected should happen, you can rest a little bit easier knowing that your résumé might need a few minor tweaks but otherwise is ready to go.

BUILD CAREER KARMA

I strongly believe in the concept of *karma*, the Buddhist belief that your actions in this life will come back to you in the next. Only, I don't think karma waits for reincarnation. I think your actions come back to you in this life, especially when it comes to your career.

The word *karma* comes from a Sanskrit word that means "action, effect, fate." Seems like a logical progression. If you're going to be proactive, you want to think about the actions you're taking, the effects you're creating, and the fate you're setting yourself up for.

The choices we make come back to us like boomerangs in very real and tangible ways. It's not by power of some mystical force; it's just the way the world works. Building career karma means recognizing this truth and doing your best to create a positive future by living a positive present.

The working world is a small place. Every day, people move around and get promoted. You never know when you're going to bump into someone you worked with years ago. Your coworker today could be your boss next year. The simple lesson? Be a nice person. Present yourself professionally to everyone. Always be polite, show respect, and act with integrity. That colleague who irritates you today could be your best client tomorrow. You just never know.

Your reputation follows you everywhere. It can be your strongest asset or your biggest liability. Once you've become known for being untrustworthy, dishonest, or unethical, the word will spread far and wide. *Remember that work is not a zero-sum game. You don't have to make others "lose" in order for you to "win."*

Finally, keep in mind that the concept of career karma isn't about doing nice things for others with the *expectation* of getting something in return.

It's about creating a professional life you can be proud of. The rewards will naturally follow if your heart is in the right place.

MANAGE STRESS

Benjamin Franklin once said, "In this world, nothing can be certain, except death and taxes."

I would add one more certainty: stress. It's an inevitable part of life for everyone. I have yet to find a stress-free working environment. Yet too many professionals fail to proactively manage stress. Instead, they reactively deal with it when it happens, and by that point, they're already suffering.

You're probably well aware of the negative impact stress can have on your life. It ravages mental, physical, social, and emotional health. Over time, it can literally kill you.

Don't wait for stress to take its painful toll. Take action now to minimize avoidable stress and manage the unavoidable. There may still be times when an acutely stressful event or situation requires more pointed action, like taking an extended leave or obtaining professional assistance. But proactive stress management will help you avoid burnout and other negative consequences caused by the accumulation of low- to mid-level chronic stress.

Being proactive in your daily work is actually a very effective form of stress management. Implementing the other strategies outlined in this book will put you far ahead of the game. Here are a few more things you can do to proactively manage stress:

- Take regular breaks throughout the day.
- Do your best to leave work on time.
- Leave work *at* work (both physically and mentally).

- Eat well and exercise regularly.
- Develop strong relationships at work.

NURTURE YOUR NETWORK

Your *professional network* is made up of the people you know and the people who know you. This group represents one of your most important career assets (second only to your strong professional reputation).

The people in your network can give you access to a whole world of opportunities that might otherwise remain out of your grasp. They can make introductions and referrals, connecting you to new people and vouching for your character and expertise. They can be a source of wisdom and information. In short, they can do for you that which you cannot do for yourself.

However, in order to effectively leverage your network, you must have strong, established relationships. This takes time and effort. When you ask people in your network for favors, you're asking them to go out on a limb for you. Most people aren't willing to put their own credibility on the line for someone they don't already know, like, and trust.

Unfortunately, a lot of professionals ignore their network until they need something. A recently launched job search inspires them to reach out for help. If you haven't contacted someone for years and you pop up out of the blue asking for favors, it doesn't create a very compelling case. It might even take the person a few minutes to remember who you are!

This is why you should always proactively nurture your network. That way, when you need something from them, they're ready to jump.

Nurturing your network doesn't take as much time as you might think. After all, people are busy. No one wants to hear from you every day or even every month. But once in a while, most people appreciate a quick email or LinkedIn message.[5] When you find a useful article that someone in your network might appreciate, send them a link with a short note: "Thought you might enjoy this! Hope you're doing well." This kind of thing positions you as a helpful resource and keeps your name top of mind.

Don't wait until you need help to show the people in your network that you care about them. Ask about their goals and offer assistance where you can. Remember, this is a two-way street. Networks are supposed to be *mutually beneficial*, meaning that both parties reap the rewards.

PROACTIVE JOB SEARCH

I would be remiss if I neglected to address the most common—and perhaps most painful—example of reactivity and its dreadful consequences in the professional world.

It's a situation I've seen play out many times over again for a great many people. See if it sounds familiar...

You're unhappy at work. No, you're actually pretty miserable. So you start a job search. The stress and anxiety of searching, combined with the frustration of your current situation, leads you to make rash decisions. You accept the first reasonable offer that comes your way. Maybe you even overlook some clear red flags about the job, but you take it anyway. And before long, you're unhappy again. No, you're actually pretty miserable. So you start yet another job search.

And thus begins a self-perpetuating cycle of misery and reactivity.

---

5 LinkedIn is the gold standard for online professional networking. If you don't have an account, get a free one *immediately*. Put together a compelling profile and start connecting with people you know, including me: Chrissy Scivicque. Visit www.EatYourCareer.com for more LinkedIn assistance if needed.

This is how job-hoppers become job-hoppers. They react to negative work situations impulsively. They don't think proactively about their next career move; they simply jump to get away from a bad situation. All too often, that leads to yet another bad situation.

Changing jobs is a natural part of career progression. Most people will do it several times in the span of one career. Gone are the days when people retire from the same company they started with immediately after college. The problem is not the job change itself. The problem is how people go about it.

Don't wait to start your job search until you're absolutely desperate to move on. Desperation yields bad decisions. Give yourself the time, space, and energy you need to weigh your options carefully. Ideally, you want to be in a position where you can afford to be picky. Get clear on what you want and don't want in your next position. Don't allow stress and anxiety to motivate you.

It is beyond the scope of this book to provide detailed guidance on the proactive job search process. However, if you're a job-hopper and you believe you're stuck in a reactive downward spiral, please take this advice to heart: *stop* the cycle. Pause and think before you take another step. Act with intention. Use the skills you've learned throughout this book to proactively choose the right path.

You can find additional resources at www.EatYourCareer.com.

CHAPTER 12

SETTING YOURSELF UP FOR SUCCESS

I am today, or some future day, what I establish today. I am today what I established yesterday or some previous day.

JAMES JOYCE, IRISH NOVELIST AND POET (1882–1941)

TEN YEARS AGO, I wrote an article for my blog called "Ten Things I'd Tell My Twenty-Three-Year-Old Self." It became, at the time, the most popular piece I had ever published online. It was the first thing I produced to ever go viral, and this was back before social media sharing became a mainstream thing. Unfortunately, the original article is no longer available online because that entire website was purchased by a company that no longer exists (but that's a story for another day).[6]

I've always been fascinated by the popularity of that article. For some reason, it struck a chord with people. Written from the perspective of my then twenty-eight-year-old self, the article shared all of the things I had learned about work and life that I wished I had known years earlier.

If I were to rewrite the article today, my now thirty-eight-year-old self would have a few choice words to add as well.

---

6 You can find a copy of the original article in the appendix.

I don't think the advice I shared is what made that article so popular. I think it was the *idea* that captured the imagination of readers around the world.

What if you could go back to your former self and share all of your hard-earned wisdom? What if future-you could tell past-you exactly what she needs to know so she can avoid the heartache of learning it on her own?

It's an interesting thought experiment, but, of course, it requires a pretty major suspension of reality. After all, there is value in doing things the hard way. If you could really circumvent the pain of the past, you wouldn't be the person you are today.

For better or worse, the you of today is a result of your past.

I still like the time machine game, though, because it reminds me that I have a responsibility. Future-me is relying on present-me. We can't go backward and do things differently, as fun as it is to imagine. All we can do is our best in this moment today. We have to try to do right by our future selves.

I want future-me, the Chrissy of tomorrow as well as the one who is forty-eight, fifty-eight, or sixty-eight years old, to look back and say, "Thank you."

Future-me will be wiser, no doubt; surely she'd have some advice for me. And there's no predicting exactly what her life will be like. But I want to do everything I can *now* to set her up for success.

I believe this is the essence of proactivity. It's about setting your future-self up for success—the you of tomorrow, the you of ten years from now and beyond. It's about creating a future in which you look back and think,

"I did everything I could." Regardless of the outcome, you didn't neglect your future. You cared for it.

THE VIRTUE OF PATIENCE

If there's one final piece of advice I can share, it's this: proactivity and patience are best friends. They're about as close as two buddies can be. In order to really be proactive, you must also have patience. It just doesn't work otherwise.

You have to be willing to do what you need to do—and keep doing it—even with no immediate return on your efforts. The payoff will come, I assure you. Please don't give up before the magic happens.

WHERE DO WE GO FROM HERE?

Throughout this book, we've walked through the proactive journey, hand in hand. Now it's time to continue the journey on your own. I must admit, as your guide in this process, I'm having a hard time letting go.

Of course, this is really just one piece of a much bigger journey—that of your career—which is, itself, only a small fraction of the epic odyssey that is life. I'm honored to have traveled with you for a while, and I hope my words serve you well as you navigate the road ahead. Perhaps our future-selves will even meet again.

My only consolation in leaving is that I've given you all I have to offer of my most cherished professional skill. There is truly nothing I value more than my ability to be proactive, and in these pages, I've held nothing back.

Nevertheless, it should be said that proactivity is not the only professional skill I cherish, nor should it be the sole focus of your professional development. Career success and, consequently, life success—however you define them—are the result of a complicated mix of ingredients. The recipe calls for so many things. *Being proactive isn't* all *you need, but it's the one thing that enhances everything else.*

Where you go from here is up to you. That's the beauty of living a proactive life. You get to choose. You have so much power if you're willing to use it.

Go on. Your future-self is waiting.

APPENDIX

READING RECOMMENDATIONS

THIS LIST INCLUDES some of my favorite books on topics related to business, communication, psychology, personal development, and more.

Change Anything: The New Science of Personal Success by Kerry Patterson, Joseph Grenny, Ron McMillan, Al Switzler, and David Maxfield

Crucial Accountability: Tools for Resolving Violated Expectations, Broken Commitments, and Bad Behavior by Kerry Patterson, Joseph Grenny, Ron McMillan, Al Switzler, and David Maxfield

Crucial Conversations: Tools for Talking When Stakes Are High by Kerry Patterson, Joseph Grenny, Ron McMillan, and Al Switzler

Getting Things Done: The Art of Stress-Free Productivity by David Allen

How Successful People Think: Change Your Thinking, Change Your Life by John C. Maxwell

How to Think Like Leonardo da Vinci: Seven Steps to Genius Every Day by Michael J. Gelb

Making It All Work: Winning at the Game of Work and the Business of Life by David Allen

No Excuses: The Power of Self-Discipline by Brian Tracy

Sway: The Irresistible Pull of Irrational Behavior by Ori Brafman and Rom Brafman

The 7 Habits of Highly Effective People: Powerful Lessons in Personal Change by Stephen R. Covey

The Compound Effect: Jumpstart Your Income, Your Life, Your Success by Darren Hardy

The Power of Habit: Why We Do What We Do in Life and Business by Charles Duhigg

The Success Principles: How to Get from Where You Are to Where You Want to Be by Jack Canfield

PROACTIVE VERSUS REACTIVE CUSTOMER SERVICE

PROACTIVE PATTY AND Reactive Rita are both schedule coordinators at a popular day spa. Let's listen in on their customer service calls, starting with Rita.

Customer: Hi, I'd like to schedule a massage please.

Rita: Of course! I actually have a 2:00 appointment available today with Mark. How does that work?

Customer: I'm not available today, unfortunately. And I'd prefer to have a female therapist if possible.

Rita: Oh, I see. What about tomorrow at 10:00 in the morning instead?

Customer: Well, I work 9:00 to 5:00, so I really need something in the evening. After 5:30 would be best.

Rita: No problem. I have a 6:00 appointment available next Wednesday with Ann.

Customer: That should work...Does Ann do deep-tissue massage?

Rita: Oh, you need deep tissue? No, let me keep looking…

Wow, this conversation is getting tedious, isn't it? Let's move on to Patty.

Customer: Hi, I'd like to schedule a massage please.

Patty: Of course! May I ask you a few questions first to better help?

Customer: Sure.

Patty: Thank you. First of all, do you have a preferred therapist?

Customer: No one specific, but I'd like a female if possible.

Patty: No problem. What type of massage do you like?

Customer: Deep tissue.

Patty: OK, and do you have a preference for day and time?

Customer: Yes, I need an appointment after 5:30 in the evening.

Patty: Perfect. Let me take a look at our schedule. (*Short pause*) I have an appointment with an amazing deep-tissue therapist named Susan at 6:00 p.m. on Friday. How does that sound?

Customer: Absolutely wonderful. Thank you!

Obviously, Patty's conversation was much more productive. Let's look at what she did right:

- Patty knew the information she needed to make the best scheduling recommendation.
- Patty got all the information up front (and asked permission to do so).
- Patty told the customer what she was doing before pausing to look at the schedule.
- Patty put together the right solution based on the full picture—she didn't just start guessing based on one piece of information.

Rita did not do any of these things and, as a result, her conversation was frustratingly unproductive for the customer.

THE 5P MODEL OF PROACTIVITY

(ORIGINALLY PUBLISHED ON *EatYourCareer.com circa 2010*)
This article represents my first attempt at creating a framework for pro-activity. It has since evolved into The Proactive Skillset, which is defined in this book.

Let's take a few minutes to look critically at your actions in the workplace.

- Do you react to the events happening around you, or do you take initiative to prepare for, participate in, and/or control the events?
- Do you take an active or passive role? Do you think in terms of the present, or do you look to the future, anticipating outcomes and preparing for the consequences?
- Do you make a decision only when you have to, when you're backed into a corner, or when you've put it off for as long as you can? Or do you make conscious decisions as part of a larger, long-term plan?

In my experience, the most valuable employees are the ones who are proactive. By definition, this means they control situations by *causing* things to happen rather than waiting to respond *after* things happen. People who are proactive don't sit around waiting for answers to appear; they stand up, put one foot in front of the other, and find the answers. They don't wait for someone to hand them an instruction manual and a box of tools; they're resourceful.

Proactive people are constantly moving forward, looking to the future, and making things happen. They're actively engaged, not passively observing. Being proactive is a way of thinking and acting.

Now, this concept can be a little abstract for some. An article written by motivational speaker Craig Harper in 2007 explains it like this:

Reactive is "I've got massive chest pain and pins and needles down my arm. Maybe I'll go to the doctor."

Proactive is "Even though I have no symptoms, I want to live a long, healthy life so I have embraced the lifelong habits of healthy eating and regular exercise."

So are you being proactive or reactive in the workplace?

Certainly, there are times when it's appropriate to be reactive. We have plenty of decisions to make in the moment. There are times when we need to be flexible and adapt to a rapidly changing environment. There are times when long-term plans must be abandoned in order to meet immediate needs. And there will always be those unavoidable roadblocks that even the most proactive person in the world would not have been able to foresee or avoid.

However, the ability to be proactive provides a clear advantage in the workplace, and most managers expect staff members to demonstrate a proactive mentality.

I have identified five key behaviors (the 5 Ps) involved in being proactive. Below, I've outlined my system and exactly how you can develop your abilities in each area.

1. PREDICT
In order to be proactive, you must first develop foresight.

Proactive people are rarely caught by surprise. Learn to anticipate problems and events. Understand how things work; look for patterns; recognize the regular routines, daily practices, and natural cycles that exist in your business. At the same time, don't allow yourself to become complacent. Use your imagination when anticipating future outcomes. Don't simply expect the past to always be an accurate predictor for the future; use your creativity and logic. Come up with multiple scenarios for how events could unfold. Proactive people are always on their toes.

2. PREVENT
Proactive people foresee potential obstacles and exert their power to find ways to overcome them before those obstacles turn into concrete roadblocks.

They prevent problems that others would simply look back on in hindsight and claim were unavoidable. Don't allow yourself to get swept up in a feeling of powerlessness. When challenges approach, take control and confront them head-on before they grow into overwhelming problems.

3. PLAN
Proactive people plan for the future.

Avoid one-step, "here-and-now" thinking, and instead, look ahead and anticipate long-term consequences. Bring the future into the present; what can you do today to ensure success tomorrow? Don't make decisions in a vacuum; every decision is a link in a chain of events leading to one final conclusion. In order to make the best decision, you have to know where you came from, where you are, and where you want to end up.

4. PARTICIPATE
Proactive people are not idle observers; they are active participants.

In order to be proactive, you must get involved. You have to take initiative and be a part of the solution. Recognize that you are only a piece of the whole and that you influence—and are influenced by—the actions of others. Don't simply react to them. Engage with them. Exert your influence and make a contribution.

5. PERFORM
Being proactive means taking timely, effective action.
You must be decisive and willing to do the work *now*. Procrastination is not an option. Take ownership of your performance and hold yourself accountable. Stand behind your decisions. Being proactive means you have taken careful, thoughtful steps to choose the appropriate path; you're not just reacting impulsively to your environment.

TEN THINGS I'D TELL MY TWENTY-THREE-YEAR-OLD SELF

(ORIGINALLY PUBLISHED ON EAToolbox.com circa 2007)
Though this article has been lightly edited to correct the most painful writing sins of the past, many still remain.

Let me first say this: I love my life. I am very happy with my job, my personal life, and who I am at this moment. I know that if I went back and changed the past, I wouldn't be where I am today, and I honestly wouldn't change a thing because of that. This post is written more as a way of organizing the lessons learned from my past. It's not meant to be a negative, remorseful account of regret. But I did learn some hard lessons—ones that I think are worth sharing here. I normally don't post things quite this personal, but it's important to me, and I hope others find something of value here.

When I was twenty-three, I was the assistant manager of a very busy financial institution. I was young to be given such a position of authority (probably *too* young), but I ran with it and did the job for just about five years before experiencing severe professional burnout. Now, several years later, I can look back on the experience and see what *really* happened. I decided to organize the many things I think I learned from my time in the bowels of corporate America by writing them down. Thus the following: a list of the ten things I'd go back and tell my twenty-three-year-old self, if only I could find a time machine to get me there.

1. Take it seriously.

I never really took my job that seriously when I was younger. I was more concerned with *life* (i.e., boys and parties). Work was always a secondary consideration. I was never that proud of my job. I lived (and still do live) in a very liberal part of liberal California. I guess I thought everyone saw bankers as being "evil" in some way, a part of corporate America, which, at the time, seemed to be the enemy for people my age. Because of that, I think I tried to make "work" a concept that existed outside of the *real* me.

If I could go back, I'd take it seriously. I wouldn't be worried about what others thought (though now I know that *I* was probably the only one judging me). I'd put in some real intellectual effort, not just the hours. I'd do the *real* work—the organizing, the planning—all the things that make a person successful. I'd do more than just "show up."

2. Be nice to people.

Probably my biggest regret is that I was (on occasion) a pretty nasty person to deal with. I guess I had a big head, being young and in charge. I was really bad at handling customer complaints. I was even worse at handling employees. I was self-consumed and, yes, a little drunk with power. If I could go back, I'd give myself a good kick in the butt—just enough to knock me into reality.

3. Watch the temper.

I'm not too proud of my lack of patience. This is one thing I've really come to value in the past few years. Patience is such an amazing virtue but very difficult for me. I'm a fast mover—an efficiency freak who loves to multitask. I am not, by nature, patient. When I was younger, I let my temper go wild, showing my lack of patience to anyone and everyone, thinking it would somehow make the world move more at my pace. Now that I've learned to control it, I realize just *how out of control* it was. I wish I could tell the younger me to relax. Things don't have to be so dramatic. I'd teach myself to meditate.

4. Get rid of the ego.

This goes back to the whole "being young and in charge" thing. I really thought I was something special. I was really just lucky. I had a big role to fill in management, and I let it go to my head. I believed I was irreplaceable, that no one could do what I did! It's silly how we think when we're young. With a little perspective, I see just how easily I could have been replaced.

5. Don't sacrifice accuracy for efficiency.

As I mentioned before, I am a fast mover. I always have been. I've always had a difficult time with waiting. I used to bring this mentality to work, thinking it was productive—*super* productive, in fact. Not true. If you're not careful, efficiency can mean sacrificing accuracy. There is a delicate balance between the two. It took a while to learn it, but now that I have, I see exactly where I went wrong in the past. I used to believe that getting things done quickly was the most important part of the process. Now I realize that getting things done right is *so much more* important!

6. Ask for help.

My ego used to get in the way of asking for help. Now I realize how critical it is to being successful in *life and work*. You just can't go it alone. You need to build a team of people around you who support your efforts. Once you find that, asking for help is essential. It's so easy to get overwhelmed by stress. Letting others help carry the burden can make all the difference. They can help get you through the tough times. Then you won't find yourself feeling overwhelmed *and alone*. At least you have people who are willing to help, if you just stand up and ask for it.

7. Take care of yourself.

I was just like every other young girl in America: I drank a little too much, and I stayed out a little too late. The sad part is, I didn't even enjoy it that much! I just thought that was what everyone else was doing. I didn't want to be left out. I always had a cold or felt tired and run down. If I had only taken care of myself, I think I would have handled the stress and heavy workload a lot better.

8. Set boundaries.

I think I allowed myself to be overworked. I never really established my limits. I just kept saying, "Yes," because I thought I was supposed to. I didn't realize that I had the right to stand up and say, "No." Creating an appropriate work-life balance is important, but it takes work. You have to set limits. When we're young, we think we have limitless energy and that we are capable of anything. This kind of thinking got me overworked and overwhelmed.

9. Don't wait for others to make things better—do it yourself.

When I was younger, I kept thinking that my boss, or his boss, should be doing something to make my job better. I never took responsibility to do it myself. Now I know that if you want something done, you have to speak up. People are busy. Take it upon yourself to make changes and improve your experience at work. Don't wait for others.

10. Get a cat.

If I could go back and find my past self, this is perhaps the most important thing I'd say: "Chrissy, you don't know it yet, but having a cat will change your life. Taking care of a sweet, cuddly little creature will make you understand the concept of being responsible for another living thing. In a weird way, it will help you take care of yourself more. It will make you love coming home at the end of a long workday. It will make you endlessly happy. It will fill your heart with warmth and love. Go get a kitty now! What are you waiting for?"

OK. Anyone know where I can find a time machine?

Note from the real Future Chrissy: Get a dog, too.

ACKNOWLEDGMENTS

THE EXPERIENCE OF writing a book is often compared to that of giving birth. It all starts with a little twinge of excitement, and it sounds so fun at first! Then, months later, as you're wallowing in pain, discomfort, and personal sacrifice, you wonder what the heck you were thinking. Ultimately, the whole ordeal culminates when your brand new baby enters the world, and you can proudly look upon it and think, "I did that."

I'm not a mother, but I can now officially say I'm a published author—and I have a whole new respect for mothers everywhere.

This book would not exist if not for the constant support, love, and encouragement of my own amazing mother. In the face of pain, discomfort, and personal sacrifice, she has always shown unyielding courage, strength, and poise. While writing this book, I often found myself silenced by self-doubt and fear; I had only to think of my mom and my voice returned. *I owe everything to her.*

I have also been blessed to have an extensive network of friends, family, and professional colleagues who have helped make this book a reality in both big ways and small. It is with deep gratitude that I express my appreciation to the following people for their specific contributions:

- To Craig, my best friend and the love of my life, for being the most patient, respectful, and supportive partner I could ever hope to have. Your impeccable work ethic and integrity inspire me every day not to settle for less in myself.

- To Dad, for helping me keep perspective and make smart business decisions.
- To my brothers and sisters, Maggie, Mark, Hunter, and Cathy, for being the kind of people I can always look up to.
- To Cathy and Mom, for reading the book prepublication and offering precious feedback and editorial corrections.
- To the boys I love most dearly, Stone, Clayton, and Reed, for filling my life with laughter and joy.
- To the girls I love most dearly, Tori and Tara, for welcoming me into your lives and hearts.
- To Julie Perrine, for inspiring me to start this adventure (and helping me actually finish it).
- To my graphic designer, Jackie Nees, who is talented beyond measure and can somehow make meaning of my scribbles.
- To my entire Orchard Club family; there are no words that accurately capture all you have done.
- To Elva, for helping to keep me sane when life got insane.
- To Dawn and Melissa, my writing sisters, for inspiring me to keep going even when it felt like trudging through quicksand.
- To all of my Eat Your Career friends, fans, and followers, for sticking with me. You've improved my life in countless ways and continue to provide me with endless inspiration. You are the reason I do what I do.

GLOSSARY

Definitions for terms included here are not intended to be comprehensive but are limited to the meaning used in this book.

action items. Things you need to do to achieve your desired results.

cognitive. Relating to or involving conscious mental activities, such as thinking, understanding, learning, and remembering.

conditions. How people are feeling, acting, and the overall atmosphere.

confidence. The willingness to improve, knowing you're capable of doing better, and believing you have the power to grow.

content. The substance; what is happening or what is being said.

context. The situation in which something happens; the group of conditions that exist.

deductive reasoning. A way of thinking that starts with a general assumption and applies it to a specific event.

desired results. Outcomes you want to create for yourself and others.

direct feedback. When someone tells you in specific terms what you need to know.

emotional intelligence. The ability to recognize and understand emotions in yourself and others, and the ability to use this awareness to manage your behavior and relationships.

goals. The combination of desired results and action items.

holistic. Complete.

humility. The ability to look at yourself honestly and see exactly what's there.

imagination. The ability to think of new things; wild and limitless.

importance. A consideration of value.

indirect feedback. When you gather clues and interpret them to determine what you need to know.

inductive reasoning. A way of thinking that starts with a specific event and creates a general assumption for the future.

industry. A group of enterprises that exist within a particular field or businesses that produce similar kinds of products or services.

influence. The capacity to have an effect on something.

initiate. To begin.

karma. The Buddhist belief that your actions in this life will come back to you in the next; from the Sanskrit word meaning action, effect, fate.

logic. A particular way of thinking; linear and limited to what we know and understand.

mutually beneficial. A relationship in which both parties reap rewards.

obstacles. Problems that stand in the way of achieving something.

opportunities. The gap between what is real and what is imagined.

outcomes. Results.

paradox. A seemingly self-contradictory situation or proposition.

pattern. A repeatable, pre-established way of doing things; a routine or sequence of events based on cause and effect.

planning. The process of regularly reviewing all of your goals and formulating strategies for achieving them.

prioritization. To determine the order for execution.

proactive. Creating or controlling a situation by causing something to happen rather than responding to it after the fact.

procedures. Applying structure to things done regularly; also system, routine, process, guideline.

professional accomplishment. Anything that adds value to the team or organization.

professional field. A group made up of individuals all engaged in the same kind of work; a group of people who possess expertise in a shared business function.

professional network. The group made up of people you know and who know you.

pull goals. A goal with action item(s) but unclear or undefined desired results.

push goals. A goal where the desired results are defined first, but you have to identify the action items to get there.

reactive. Acting in response to a situation rather than creating or controlling it.

safety margin. Additional buffer added to time estimates to account for the unexpected.

synergy. An interaction wherein the whole is greater than the sum of its parts.

synthesize. To process and create meaning from.

team. The group of people with whom you work cooperatively to accomplish a shared set of goals.

urgency. A consideration of time.

whole-self observation. The ability to see, hear, and even feel what is happening around you and within you.

BRING THE PROACTIVE JOURNEY TO YOUR ORGANIZATION

"Regardless of what you do for a living, being proactive is the most essential (and underutilized) tool for professional empowerment and personal productivity."

CHRISSY SCIVICQUE

You've already been inspired by the book; now you can take your learning even deeper and help others experience the incredible benefits of being proactive too.

- Help your entire organization get ahead of the competition.
- Raise the bar for your whole team.
- Create a forward-thinking culture of accountability.
- Set yourselves up for future success.

Experience *The Proactive Journey* onsite, live, and in person with master trainer Chrissy Scivicque and feel the powerful shift firsthand.

- Increase productivity.
- Improve resourcefulness.
- Prevent and minimize problems.
- Experience greater control and less stress.

In training, you'll get even more…

- real-world application strategies
- case studies and examples
- lively discussion and group work

This eight-hour interactive workshop can also be customized for roles and teams:

- The Proactive Sales Professional
- The Proactive Customer Service Representative
- The Proactive Administrative Professional
- The Proactive Trainer
- The Proactive Manager
- The Proactive Leader
- The Proactive Team
- The Proactive Organization

All workshops are tailored for your organization and group. Pricing and availability information are available via phone or email. Contact Chrissy@ EatYourCareer.com to learn more.

> *"Chrissy has a unique ability to inspire, engage, and motivate audiences of all ages and backgrounds. She provides quality information and fresh ideas in an entertaining, fast-paced format. I never hesitate to attend training offered by Chrissy because I know the time will be well spent. I am happy to recommend her."*
>
> VP MARKETING AND PUBLIC RELATIONS, ILD COMMUNICATIONS

Made in the USA
Las Vegas, NV
15 October 2021

32416924R00115